Deborah Olson details the anatomy of friendship and explains how these components work to strengthen bonds and create flow. Research shows that our happiness correlates to our social relationships; so does our health. This book is a delightful road map to cultivate and nurture our circle of connections. *The Healing Power of Girlfriends* is an engaging, upbeat, and inspiring five-star read.

Laurie Buchanan, PhD
holistic health practitioner, transformational life coach, and award-winning author

As a psychologist, I *love* that *The Healing Power of Girlfriends* evolves from a combination of theory and research. Deborah Olson's concentric circle theory makes the importance of the levels of friendship obvious and easy to understand. Her passion for the importance of these relationships to the physical and mental health of women is evident.

Marsha J. Harman, PhD
professor of psychology, Sam Houston State University

Deborah Olson has gifted us with an articulate, practical guide about the power of female friendship! This book is a must-read adjunct to her body of work. By peeling back the layers of important relationships in women's lives and using the "Olson Friendship Framework," she has provided a structure to understanding our relationships over the years with female friends and working colleagues.

As a nurse and leader, I believe that the Olson framework adds an insightful dimension to working with women colleagues and patients in the healthcare environment.

The greatest gift from this author is encouraging us to accept that some relationships are meant to be there to serve us during specific phases of our lives.

Cas Luis, MSN, RN

Being a good friend is being a good person: making time for others, really listening to them, keeping their secrets. In *The Healing Power of Girlfriends*, Deborah Olson will inspire you to nurture those relationships—and be a better friend to yourself in the process.

Maureen Anderson
host of the *Doing What Works* nationally syndicated radio talk show

In *The Healing Power of Girlfriends*, Deborah Olson celebrates one of the most significant, yet often overlooked, relationships: female friendships. Packed with inspiration, insights, and personal stories, this book captures the nuances and uniqueness of the bonds that only exist within friendships between women—friendships that, according to research, have powerful and lasting effects on our health, happiness, and overall well-being. Reading this book will give you a renewed appreciation for your female friendships.

Allison Abrams, LCSW-R
psychotherapist, author, and contributing expert for
Psychology Today and *The Huffington Post*

THE
Healing Power
OF
Girlfriends

THE
Healing Power
OF
Girlfriends

How to Create Your Best Life
Through Female Connection

DEBORAH A. OLSON, RN, MA, LPC

GALLERIA
COUNSELING & CONSULTING
"Well Living for Living Well"

The Healing Power of Girlfriends
How to Create Your Best Life Through Female Connection

© 2019 Deborah A. Olson, RN, MA, LPC

The information provided in this book is for general information purposes only. It is not intended as a substitute for advice from a licensed therapist. The methods described are the author's personal thoughts and are not intended to be a definitive set of instructions.

Cover design by Jera Publishing
Interior design by Jera Publishing
Author photo by Pat Guard, Pat & Ray's Studio,
Kingwood, Texas
Edited by Candace Johnson, Change It Up Editing

Poem on page 118 reprinted with permission of
DOGEARED® Jewelry

ISBN: 978-1-7337010-0-6

Published by:
Galleria Publishing
4265 San Felipe St.
Suite #1100
Houston, Texas 77027

Dedicated with love to all of my amazing girlfriends who have played a part in my life journey and left their lasting imprint on my soul. And to my dear friends mentioned in this book who have gone on to receive their true angel wings, I dedicate this work of love to your treasured memory, forever tucked away in my thankful heart.

CONTENTS

ACKNOWLEDGMENTS

Since I was a young child, I have had the dream of one day writing and publishing a book. This dream has finally become reality with the help and dedication of many special people.

First, my deep gratitude to all of my girlfriends who have been the driving force behind my passion to put into words and share with the world that life is richer, better, happier, healthier, and longer when we embrace our female friendships. To all of you who have cried with me during the difficult times, laughed with me during the joyous times, and encouraged and supported me when I needed it most, you are truly my earthly angels.

Thank you to all of my female clients who have trusted me enough to share their vulnerabilities and their stories. I am very proud of the work we have done together and grateful for the opportunity you have given me to learn more about the unique connections of your female friendships.

A big shout out to my fabulous friends in many states who took the time out of their busy lives to distribute my Female Friendship Questionnaires, and to all the wonderful ladies of MOPS, church groups, and book clubs who filled them out.

This truly was a labor of love on your part, and it has greatly enriched this book. I am forever grateful.

Special gratitude goes to my former graduate school professor, Dr. Marsha Harman, who is now not only my trusted colleague but most importantly a dear friend. Marsha, your perspective has always been a breath of fresh air, and you helped me believe in myself when I was losing my way.

And in a league by herself is Candace Johnson, my editor, mentor, coach, and, after many months of working together, a treasured and dear friend. Candace, you have walked alongside me this past year during what has been the most challenging year of my life due to my husband's health issues. But through it all, you helped me weather the storms and stay the course. You always seemed to know just what I needed, and provided humor when I needed a chuckle, a pat on the back when I was discouraged, and a little gentle nudge when I needed to get going. Your expertise, knowledge, and insight have been gifts beyond measure. As I have told you many times, you are the wind beneath my wings, and I am so honored to have had you as my copilot on this first flight. I am eternally grateful to you, Candace!

I would like to also thank Cindy Barrilleaux, who did the first round of edits on the rough draft of this book. I promised you, Cindy, that I would come to New Mexico and place a copy of this in your hands one day. Here I come!

My special thanks and deep gratitude to my colleague and friend Kimberly Campbell (QUEST Business Strategies), who shared her brilliant and creative ideas in our collaborative efforts to design a unique paradigm for female friendships. You brought my theories and visions to life, Kimberly, and took them from my head and into the world of artistic visual tools where women everywhere can now benefit from them.

To Merlin Clarke and Marcia Maizel-Clarke, owners of DOGEARED® Jewelry, my special thanks for your beautiful anchor necklace creation that brings joy to all of us. It's a visual reminder of the opportunity we have to be someone's anchor in our female friendships. My gratitude to you for graciously allowing me to feature your poem "Friendship" in my book.

A special nod to author and naturalist Dr. Rachel Cartwright, who I had the privilege of meeting on our Princess cruise to Alaska in the summer of 2018. What a joy it was to discuss the behaviors of female humpbacks after your lecture. Thank you, Rachel, for sharing your passion of the amazing humpbacks with me and for supporting my passion to promote the healing power of girlfriends.

Thank you to Ingrid Noe, my talented website designer, graphic artist, and friend. Ingrid, your creations have always been innovative, beautiful, and exceptional. I am forever grateful for your faithful support and for always creating the perfect graphics and designs to help me build a successful business and push on toward my dreams.

To my social media expert, Sue Canfield, thank you from the bottom of my heart for your stellar efforts to bring the news of my first book to the world through social media. You and your team are exceptional and visionary, and I cannot imagine the past several months preparing for this book launch without you on board.

And, to everyone at Jera Publishing—especially Kimberly, Jason, and Stephanie—my sincere gratitude for all you have done to bring this "baby" to life. Jason, thanks for sharing your talents to create the perfect book cover, and getting everything on that beach scene just perfect. You are the best! Stephanie, thank you for an incredible interior design. You did an awesome job with all my graphics and reproducing the diagrams, making them easy to read and enjoy! Kimberly, your support and mentoring with the publishing process was invaluable! Your guidance for this newbie author was exactly what I needed to get me to the finish line!

To the love of my life for 40 years, my husband, Dave, thank you for pushing through your health struggles of this past year so that you can be here with us today to celebrate our growing family! We are all very aware that you are a walking miracle, and we are very grateful you are a fighter and on the road to recovery! Your continued support, encouragement, and love through my many years of education, and now this book project, have meant more to me than words can say. Thank you for sharing my dreams and helping to make them come true!

To my four adult kids, Brandi, Brooke, Ben, and Brett, and their spouses, Beto, Katie, and Alan, thank you for your love, inspiration, and cheering me on. Ben, your advice and knowledge on marketing and launching my book have been invaluable! Brett, you are still the most patient and helpful tech guy on the planet; thank you for sharing your skills with me! Brandi, Brooke, and Katie, thank you for sharing the amazing gift of female friendship with me! To my five precious grandbabies, Evie, Charlotte, Alessandra, Alberto Patrick, and Sienna, you all have helped me get in touch with my younger self again, finding the wonder and awe in the little things in life, and for that, my cup runneth over.

And, to the One who makes all things possible, I am forever grateful for the many gifts of this life. I truly take nothing for granted. Thanks be to our God who created us for connection so that we can enjoy the benefits of the healing power of girlfriends.

INTRODUCTION

Women's health has always been my passion. My excitement was first ignited in 1976 at Nebraska Methodist Hospital School of Nursing (today called Nebraska Methodist College of Nursing), when I decided to follow my heart for helping women by pursuing a career in obstetrics (OB) and gynecology (GYN). Although I found all specialty areas fascinating, as we moved through our different nursing rotations, nothing equaled the passion I felt for helping women, whether it was partnering with them through their hours of labor, providing bedside care on the postpartum unit, tending to a patient on the gynecological unit, or working on the high-risk OB floor for pregnant moms-to-be. Following graduation from nursing school, I quickly found my niche, and I started working as a registered nurse (RN) at Methodist Hospital in Omaha.

One of my favorite parts of my job was the time spent giving emotional support at the bedside. It was soon apparent to me how therapeutic it can be for women to share during times of illness and stress. From comforting a new mom during the emotionally charged days on the postpartum unit to encouraging a pregnant mom who was hospitalized for complications, the chats we shared are some of my most significant memories of my nursing career. I saw an opportunity to provide emotional healing in those moments through listening, affirming, validating, and encouraging. We connected woman-to-woman because there seemed to be an innate bond hardwired within us.

Several years later, after taking a "pause" from nursing to build my own nest of babies (I gave birth to four babies in seven years), I found myself longing to return to this passion and to make a difference in women's lives. However, I felt drawn toward learning more about the emotional side of health care, which led me to pursue a bachelor's degree in psychology. After completion, I entered graduate school and earned a master's degree in clinical psychology from Sam Houston State University in Huntsville, Texas. It was not an easy mountain to climb for this mother of four who, because of my husband's demanding career, was in essence a "single mom" the majority of the time. But my desire to help women kept the fires lit beneath me, and despite the challenges, quitting never was an option.

And now, I have been working with women—from teenagers to the elderly—in my private practice as a licensed professional counselor (LPC) in the greater Houston, Texas area for nearly two decades. I have received numerous postgraduate certifications in postpartum and pregnancy emotional health. As a specialist in this area, I have conducted weekend seminars and workshops for women on various topics related to emotional health, with titles such as "Nourish to Flourish," "Productivity and Positivity," "Happiness & Longevity," and "The Healing Power of Girlfriends." I have written and published articles on these relevant topics with the hope that lives will be touched and emotional healing will begin.

My ambition to write this book springs from years of working with many female clients and learning about the dynamics of female friendships, which are unique from other relationships. Women connect in ways that men and women do not typically relate. As women, we need to talk, and we thrive on connecting through verbally sharing with other women, or as some have said, "we engage in verbal vomiting." Both leading women's support groups and counseling women have given me a front row seat in observing the potential healing that can occur through female bonds. I have witnessed a metamorphosis occur in these support groups as women find the courage to break out of their old selves and dare to find stronger, and more resilient and empowered, new versions of themselves.

For the past six years, I have been researching female friendships, with a special emphasis on what is healing about having girlfriends. Recently, I collected my own data. Through designing a questionnaire on friendship, which I distributed to women across the United States, I have gained the perspective of many women on the merits of friendship, and I am excited to share this revealing information with you. This one-page survey included five questions about female friendship as well as a demographics box to check for the participant's age group. Questionnaires were disseminated to women in ten states from coast to coast and were mailed back to my office mailbox. Between December 2017 and April 2018, nearly 150 women returned their completed surveys.

One of the triggering events that put this book into motion came unexpectedly a few years ago, while I was sitting on a beach in Mexico. My husband, Dave, and I were on a summer vacation with Kathy and Harlan, another couple with whom we have had a close friendship for over 35 years (despite living across the country for most of those years). On the beach that day, my girlfriend and I began discussing our own friendship, and how it had survived over the years as we raised children, pursued our careers, and lived great distances apart.

As the day progressed and we started examining this special bond more closely, Harlan shared his perspective with us. He commented that despite the miles, and sometimes the years, that would separate us, both of us stayed in close touch and held tight to our special friendship. He asked us what we thought was the secret to that success, considering that we all live in a frenetic world that robs us of time to invest in building and maintaining friendships. Kathy and I looked at each other and smiled. We were thinking the same thing.

"You know," I said, "I would have to say it was our unspoken commitment to the friendship and how much it meant to both of us. We had such a solid and special friendship already established before my move to Texas in 1992, and we both felt strongly that we did not want to see this relationship end."

Our relationship had begun in 1981, when we both moved to Milwaukee from out of state for our husbands' careers. Our husbands were both gone a lot pursing their medical careers, which left us essentially as single parents much of the time.

My only child was about to turn one, and Kathy was pregnant and almost ready to deliver their first baby. We bonded immediately because we both were longing for our families back home and needing to share motherhood with a new friend. The rest is history. Our friendship now spans more than three decades.

"Remember," Kathy added, "I told you how the day after the moving van drove away and you were gone, I pulled into your driveway and just sat in my car looking at your empty house—and I burst into tears!"

"Yes," I replied, "I still get choked up when I think of you sitting there crying."

"The memories came flooding back to me: all the years with the kids, the birthdays, the holidays, and the special times we had shared together," she continued. "We were family, and we were there for each other no matter what. None of us had relatives close or even in the same state."

"You are so right, Kathy," I recalled. "I remember you always would say, 'Our friends are the family we have *chosen*,' and we could not have been more like a family if we had been blood relatives! We knew we would spring into action quickly for each other."

Kathy smiled and replied, "Yes, that was always my mantra, and still is today. Remember the time you and Dave and the kids came over to our house for Thanksgiving dinner and I had become very sick earlier that day and ended up in bed? You stepped into action along with Harlan and Dave and finished up the dinner preparations for me. Everyone, except me, still got their holiday turkey feast, the kids were happy, and we did not miss a beat!" At this memory, we both chuckled as that was a rather unusual Thanksgiving, and a testament to the level of intimacy of our shared friendship. Truly, a family is what we were and still are today.

"I clearly remember opening the mailbox to see the first letter I received after our move to Texas, which was a letter from you," I responded. "As I sat down to read it, I broke down and started crying. I asked myself what we had done by moving halfway across the country and leaving beloved friendships behind. But in that defining moment, I also told myself, with the determination of steel, 'I will not let distance rob me of my special sisterhood with my dear friend. I will find a way to make this work, to stay in touch, to stay close in heart, and to keep our connection alive, so help me God.'"

That conversation on the beach left us both with a new and fresh appreciation for the depth and the strength of our long friendship, which initially provided us with a lifeline to a support system and a connection to another person who was living the same reality and understood the challenges, frustrations, and emotions. We "got" each other as only female friends do.

Kathy and I soon became friends with two other young women, Beth and Jody, whose husbands also worked in emergency medicine with our husbands, and who also had moved in from out of state. The four of us found many common threads in our lives as women, wives, and moms. We celebrated the best of times together and were committed to our unique and special friendships throughout the years. Distance, time, money, and raising busy families limited our meetups, but we stayed connected despite all odds.

Fast forward a few decades, and we had decided to plan our first-ever girlfriend weekend in Florida. We walked the beach, lay by the pool, shopped, shared some wine, and ate delicious seafood. We watched some great movies, most notably *Divine Secrets of the Ya-Ya Sisterhood*, and quickly decided we needed to have a name for the four of us. What better name could there be than the Ya-Yas? So that is what we tagged our sisterhood, and that is what we are still to this day!

Since that trip, the Ya-Yas have made several more girlfriend trips together, and we still stay in touch regularly. We share a long history that spans more than 30 years and many states. Our love and commitment to each other has never waned. No matter what life brings us, we offer solid support to each other. The souls we have bared and shared with each other over the years are richer for the connection we have known as the Ya-Ya sisterhood.

I will be forever grateful to God for placing these Ya-Ya girlfriends in my life as well as for the many other special friends that I will be mentioning later in this book. They have all played a special part in sparking my interest in the merits of female friendships. I am passionate about celebrating and embracing the gift of girlfriends and how those girlfriends enrich life beyond measure. Writing this book has come from a place deep in my heart, a place that is filled with the joy, treasures, and memories collected from decades with my soul sisters. My personal mission is to strike a chord with women everywhere and awaken them to the powerful gift and benefits of female friendship.

In my clinical practice as a therapist, I have worked with all types of women from a variety of demographics. In the end, what I have learned is that all women are connected by a thread woven deep into the core of our souls. We are made by our creator to hunger for many of the same things, feel a wide spectrum of emotions in a similar way, and struggle through comparable challenges, all the while searching for connection. In the end, we are much the same. Research studies point to what many of us have concluded from life experience: we are happier and healthier when we share close connections with other women.

We are united by the bond of womanhood and a universal experience of what it means to have female friendships. The empirical evidence is solid: there are emotional, mental, and physical benefits that are connected with having close girlfriends.

I've also learned that not all levels of friendship are equal in terms of their definition, depth, longevity, attributes, and intimacy. There are many ways to conceive of the varying intimacy levels in relationships. To capture this phenomenon, I've created a visual paradigm called the "Olson Friendship Framework" (learn more in Chapter 3), which will lend clarity and highlight the differences. This framework will serve to enrich and embellish our understanding of girlfriend relationships and our expectations at varying levels of friendship.

I have also provided discussion questions at the end of the chapters. These questions offer a format for discussion in book clubs, church groups, Bible studies, educational classes for women, and other venues where women gather together.

It is my hope that through reading these pages and pondering the dynamics and merits of girlfriend relationships, more women will seize the opportunities they have to participate in female friendships. We have been created biologically to gather with our girlfriends, and when we do, we reap a myriad of powerful health benefits. This book was written for all women everywhere, and it is the culmination of my professional and personal experiences through the decades of my life as a woman, nurse, mental health clinician, mother, wife, and friend. My lifelong desire to improve women's health has been the motivation that has kept me on the path toward getting this book into your hands. Unlike many previous and excellent books on female friendships, this book uniquely advocates for:

The Healing Power of Girlfriends!

$\mathscr{C}$1

$\mathscr{W}$hat Is $\mathscr{F}$riendship?

> We have found that friendships between women are deeper, more enduring, and more plentiful than those between men.
>
> **Joel Block and Diane Greenberg,**
> *Women and Friendship*

$\mathbf{T}$he concept of friendship exists as a unique paradigm, distinct from other relationships we participate in during our lifetime. In this relationship, the connection is not formed through the bonds of marriage or blood relation. That said, a mother-daughter or sister-sister bond will often operate much like a female friendship. However, one of the hallmark features of friendship is that we share the bond on the premise that we are willing to both give and receive with each other—not out of duty, but because we choose to be in the relationship. This creates a reciprocal quality to the relationship that makes it distinct and sets it apart from spousal or familial relationships.

The definitions of "friendship" vary, but there are many common traits that remain constant and similar themes in what people look for and expect from someone they consider a friend. GoodTherapy.org defines friendship as "a close association between two people marked by feelings of care, respect, admiration, concern, love, or like." Much has been written over the years about the concept of friendship. Aristotle said, "True friendship is lasting because it is grounded in good." This quote perfectly highlights what is at the core of an authentic friendship. The foundational building blocks of a true friendship are comprised of a solid, shared commitment to the betterment of the other. It is this core connection that defines and shapes the relationship and creates an environment of safety, authenticity, and vulnerability.

There are many different levels of friendships, and as such, the depth of the relationship varies as well. We tend to show more vulnerability with those friendships in which we feel safe and accepted. In more superficial relationships, we often share only a small portion of ourselves as a way of protecting our hearts.

Our friendships are as individual as the people who are in them. I consider myself very blessed to have many girlfriends, and the relationship I have with each one is special and unique. There are many factors that come into play with these friendships, which gives each relationship its distinctive flavor and individual quality. My Ya-Ya friendships are a perfect example to illustrate this point.

Beth brings a warm and caring heart to the table of friendship. She loves to help people and make a difference. For many years, Beth provided highly skilled and loving care as an RN in the neonatal intensive care unit (NICU), and so we share that nursing connection, wanting to heal those in need. If you ever need a favor, Beth is there, and she will give you the shirt off her back to help out. Beth's compassion for others is a core part of who she is as a nurse and as a friend!

Jody possesses a high-energy and vibrant passion for family, friends, and living a healthy lifestyle, and she has a love for nature. When our kids were young, she hosted some amazing family parties for all of us at her country home near Milwaukee. Jody brings many special assets to our Ya-Ya friendship, including strength, resilience, empowerment, and a "can-do" approach to life. You feel all of those traits when you are in her presence, and they do rub off on you! She has a dedication and loyalty to her close friends that is evidenced by her unconditional love for all of us Ya-Ya sisters.

Kathy adds a sweet breath of fresh air, imbued with a fun sense of humor, that keeps all of us from taking life or ourselves too seriously. She is for sure the least intense of the four of us, and thus adds some levity and lightheartedness to our friendship table. Her heart for others is huge, kind, and loving. When life's curveballs start getting tossed your direction, you know she will always be there for you, no matter what! Kathy brings a special quality of thoughtfulness to our group, and often one of us will find a note of encouragement from her in the mailbox on a day when we need it most.

I cherish each relationship with my gal pals and celebrate each one for the special part it plays in my life journey. In Chapter 3, much more will be shared on the different levels of friendships and how they give structure and definition to the types of relationships we participate in with our girlfriends.

Over the years, I have offered many workshops, seminars, and weekend retreats for women on a variety of topics. Recently I have been speaking on friendships and asking women what they seek in a friendship. I've found that women generally want similar things in their girlfriend relationships.

I ask these women the question, "What are your expectations in female friendships with your girlfriends?" This opens up a plethora of conversations and ideas on the qualities women are looking for and value in their friendships. There are definitely common themes in their answers, such as loyalty, honesty, connecting on a soul level, mutual respect, acceptance, availability to spend time together, and holding the same values and ideals, to name a few. It makes sense that as we go through different life stages and chapters, our priorities change as well, and what we emphasize or value in a friendship may shift. However, as I have worked with many different women through the years who are at various stages of life, I have seen several unifying threads in what they continue to value and seek in friendships.

Female Friendship Questionnaire

In trying to gain a deeper understanding of what women really are searching for in female friendships, I designed and distributed the "Female Friendship Questionnaire" to tap into some of the core expectations, values, and perspectives that women share. This five-question survey was sent to women who range from 20 to 60 years of age and live in nine states, from the eastern coast of Florida to the northwest coast of Oregon. I definitely saw trends in the answers, which I'll share throughout this book.

Let's examine the definition of friendship first.

GALLERIA
COUNSELING & CONSULTING
"Well Living for Living Well"

Female Friendship Questionnaire

Based on your experience with female friends, please answer the following questions. Your answers will remain anonymous. Participation in this project is optional and much appreciated.

Please check your age group for our demographics information:
___ 20 to 30 ___ 31 to 40 ___ 41 to 50 ___ 51 to 60 ___ 61 and over

What does friendship mean to you?

What are your expectations of female friendships?

What do you think you bring to your friendships with other women?

All things being equal, is there anything you would like to be different in any of your female friendships?

What do you see as the benefits for you from friendships with women?

What Is "Friendship"?

What friendship means for so many of us seems to cross all demographics, including age and geography. Many women defined friendship as a safe place to "be me and share my heart." They also described friendship as a bond, as being loyal, and as having joint interests and weathering the ups and downs of life. Other responses included defining friendship as companionship, giving and receiving support, and having a no-judgment zone where you can be yourself. I saw strong parallels across all age groups for how women defined friendship and the essential traits of a meaningful connection. Here is a sample of some of their responses (followed by age range in parentheses):

"Friendship means leaning in. Being 100 percent honest. Friendship to me is emotional. If I'm not emotionally connected, I tend not to be a 'good' friend" (31–40 years old).

"Being able to confide my joys and hopes, the secrets of my heart, my fears and insecurities, or even complain without fear of judgment. And friendship means being able to laugh, play, and share my childlike side freely. It is growing old together as we become women of wisdom and grace" (61+ years old).

"Deep friendships are those girded in honesty and sacrifice, with freedom to share and hold each other accountable and give up one's own desires to help" (31–40 years old).

"Friendship means you can count on them and they can count on you. It is a FAMILY BY CHOICE, but family nonetheless" (31–40 years old).

"Friends are women I can laugh and cry with in the same conversation. Friends come in all shapes and sizes, but the friends I cherish are the ones who I feel love me for being me and whom I love unconditionally" (61+ years old).

When looking at what we seek in our female friends, we must consider the actual expectations we bring to the table of friendship. Since we each have a unique history, our expectations for friendships are connected to and defined by life experiences. Thus, our expectations require deliberate examination because they play a part in how we view ourselves and others in the friendship.

How Expectations Define Friendship

Our life journeys, and the experiences we have had, shape us as individuals and color the way we view ourselves and others. One of the places this comes to light is in our friendships, and in the expectations we bring to those relationships.

We know that when two people have similar expectations and ideas for what they want and need in the friendship, the relationship will most likely develop into a positive and meaningful experience for both. This friendship is especially likely to grow if both people are at similar places in their life journeys or are seeking a relatively equal level of friendship at the same time.

It is also in these expectations that we can get set up for disappointment, frustration, and problems in the friendship. This may result when two people have a different set of ideas about what friendship looks like, or what they need out of it.

Our expectations are also a product of where we are in life and what circumstances we are dealing with at the time. Many women over the years have shared with me how their expectations for the relationship contrasted sharply with those of their girlfriend, which ultimately either changed or ended the friendship. At one of my women's seminar weekend retreats, one of the participants shared her own emotional friendship struggle with our group. She told a story of how different expectations can play a critical part in our friendships.

I was at a point in my life where I was looking for and needing a new friend. One of my dear friends had recently moved out of state, and I was feeling that loss very deeply. A new family had just moved into our neighborhood, and I was eager to introduce myself to the wife in hopes that maybe this would be a lady I could connect with. Over the next few months, I reached out numerous times and set up lunch dates to meet her, and I tried to be helpful to set up play dates for our kids. I really wanted to make this a special friendship and did everything I could to be available and connect with her. Sometimes she was able to meet me for lunch, but most often, she had an excuse that she was busy, or had a conflict that day. As time passed, it became clear to me that she was not all that interested in sharing a friendship. Her lack of interest in participating in the new friendship was puzzling to me, and I experienced this as rejection, which was also hurtful. Before long, she actually put her cards on the table and was completely honest with me. She told me she knew her husband's job would take them away on another move within the year, [and] she did not have the time or the energy to invest in a friendship. Although I was sad to hear they would be leaving the neighborhood soon, I was also very relieved that none of this was actually about me. I had been taking this rejection so personally and wondering what she found so unacceptable in me as a new friend, or what I had done to make her stay so aloof and unavailable. Now I can see it all for what it really was. This new neighbor was only protecting herself from getting attached to a new friend that she would only have to soon say good-bye to once again. It had nothing to do with me, and everything to do with her!

This story demonstrates so clearly how we bring our own personal set of expectations to the friendship circle. Timing can be critical to the development of a friendship, and if people are at different points in their lives with situations that are not really parallel, the relationship may not develop. The result can be disappointment, conflict, emotional struggles, and ultimately, a potential loss of the friendship. What is essential to remember is that there are numerous factors at play that impact the success or failure of the friendship. It is human to feel rejected and to start second-guessing yourself as you try to find a valid reason why this person does not seem interested in developing a friendship with you. In reality, this causes distress and angst that we could probably avoid by reminding ourselves that it isn't always about us and our "stuff." Sometimes, it is about the other person and her "stuff."

This powerful concept of expectations in friendship, and the implications that result, will be explored in more depth in the coming chapters as we delve into the "Olson Friendship Framework" and the different attributes of friendships that exist within varied circles of friends. When there are significant differences in how you and your friend perceive your relationship, "danger zones" can result, leading to awkwardness, conflicts, and disappointments. Learning how to spot these danger zones before they become an issue is worth examining in more detail and will be addressed as we explore the friendship framework.

In summary, there are many parallels in how women define female friendship and what they value and desire in the relationship. There are several universal traits of friendship and common threads across all age groups. Our expectations may be colored by numerous factors, including our life circumstances and the timing constraints that result. However, across the life span, most women's expectations tend to be more similar than different. As females, we value a place to be ourselves without judgment, the freedom to be authentic without fear of rejection, and the opportunity to be loved unconditionally and to feel accepted by a loyal friend who is honest and trustworthy, always.

DISCUSSION QUESTIONS

1. How do you define "female friendship," and how has your definition changed as you have had more life experiences?

2. What are your expectations from your female friendships? (Examples include loyalty, respect, honesty, sense of humor, and like-mindedness.)

3. How do those traits contribute to the connection you feel in the friendship? Discuss a time when you realized the expectations for the friendship were very different than those of your girlfriend.

   a) How did you navigate through this challenge?

   b) Did the friendship survive this challenge? Explain.

   c) What are some things you learned about friendship after going through this experience?

4. My research has found that a common thread among women is a desire to be in a friendship that is a "judgment-free zone." In what ways does that help make the relationship connection stronger and more valuable for you?

5. Most women seem to want a girlfriend they can confide in while knowing this friend will keep their secrets confidential. Can you discuss a time when a friend betrayed your confidence?

    a) How did this betrayal change how you shared confidential information, and were you able to trust again in the next friendship?

6. Think of a friendship that you have been in that has spanned years or even decades. How has the relationship changed, and/or grown deeper or stronger, by the experiences you have been through as female friends?

    a) What were some of the key factors in the friendship that survived the test of time and the trials of life?

    b) How were you able to work through challenges that presented in the friendship?

2

Girlfriends Connect Us to Health, Happiness, and Longevity

Everything in life that truly matters can be boiled down to relationships.

Gary Smalley,
The DNA of Relationships

Numerous published studies and articles clearly support the argument that there are health benefits for having a circle of supportive friends. Research suggests that when we have meaningful friendships, we also experience greater happiness in our lives and enjoy lower stress levels as well as have faster recovery rates from surgery, fewer diseases, and greater chances of reaching life goals.

We can see this in the way my mother-in-law navigated her way through becoming a young widow when she was in her early forties, with three children to support and raise alone. She quickly made her plan to move ahead to provide for her children with her full-time job as a nurse, while making her house payments so the family did not have to move. When I asked her many years ago how she managed to keep going through those dark days, she shared that the ability to function on a daily basis was due to the love and support she received from her circle of close friends in her small, tight-knit Nebraska town. She also credited her dedicated extended family who lived in nearby Kansas with lending essential support during those difficult years. In addition, her connections with her two sisters served as deep friendships that she treasured. She went on to successfully launch all three children to college and live a long and fairly healthy life, well into her mid-nineties. She is a perfect example of how the connection of friendship can help us live healthier, happier, and longer lives, despite some of the biggest challenges.

What Scientific Research Tells Us About the Importance of Friendships

For nearly two decades, scientists have been examining how friendships correlate with our health outcomes, and the findings connecting them continue to be robust. In an article by social psychologist David G. Myers titled "The Funds, Friends, and Faith of Happy People," published in the January 2000 edition of *American Psychologist*, researchers' findings were that age, gender, and income give little clue to a person's level of happiness. Instead, better predictors of happiness come from having a network of close relationships and a faith that embraces social support, purpose, and hope (Myers, 2000, 56–67).

All friendships matter, but a landmark UCLA study in 2000 suggests that friendships between women are special. UCLA psychologists Shelley Taylor, PhD, and Laura Cousino Klein,

PhD, along with their research team, examined hundreds of biological and behavioral studies on the stress response in humans and animals. Their analysis suggests that the modified stress response in females results in affiliation and relaxation, which Dr. Taylor coined as "tend and befriend" (Taylor et al, 2000, 411–429).

Instead of exhibiting the fight-or-flight response as men typically do, women release oxytocin when they are stressed. This release buffers the fight-or-flight response and encourages them to tend to children and gather with friends instead. When women engage in tending or befriending, additional oxytocin is released, which further counters stress and produces a calming effect. This calming response does not happen for men; the high levels of testosterone produced when they are stressed reduce the oxytocin benefits.

Women's notion to tend and befriend may minimize their vulnerability to a wide variety of stress-related disorders, including those tied to diseases of the cardiovascular system; this may be one reason why, according to Dr. Taylor and Dr. Klein, women outlive men by an average of 7.5 years. These scientists also referenced a 1988 study published in the *Annual Review of Sociology* showing that important benefits result from positive physical contact—like hugging, touching, and cuddling—as it causes a release of stress-decreasing oxytocin. They concluded that this social support may offer health protection by countering the stress response in the body, resulting in relaxation (House et al, 1988, 293–318).

Other studies reveal that friendship is likely to have an even greater effect on a woman's health than her relationship with her spouse, significant other, and/or a family member. A 2006 study published in the *Journal of Clinical Oncology* looked at 3,000 nurses with breast cancer and found that women without close friends were four times as likely to die from the disease as women with at least ten friends. Having a spouse did not correlate with survival rates (Kroenke et al, 2006, 1105–1111).

According to David Spiegel, MD, renowned psychiatrist at Stanford University, we are wired to be social creatures, and it is that social connection that has enabled us to survive on this planet so successfully since the beginning of time. Dr. Spiegel believes that being connected to others is key when we face illness because it helps us manage our stress responses. This connection to others allows our bodies to do better and lends us valuable emotional support as we face life-threatening situations (Spiegel, 2014).

We know women connect with each other very differently than men do. In an article on Healthline.com, Alisa Ruby Bash, PsyD, LMFT, is quoted as saying, "Research shows that women, [possibly] more than men, need to maintain those connections. It increases serotonin and oxytocin, the bonding hormone" (Barcella, 2017).

In a 2010 Brigham Young University (BYU) meta-analytic review, researchers Julianne Holt-Lunstad, PhD, Timothy B. Smith, PhD, and J. Bradley Layton, PhD, examined 150 longitudinal studies on how the frequency of human interactions affects health outcomes. They found that feeling disconnected from friends is twice as dangerous as obesity. In fact, this study concluded that having supportive and connected friendships improves our odds of survival by 50 percent. This means that our social connections are a significant and essential part of the formula that determines our longevity (Holt-Lunstad et al, 2017, 517–530).

Several articles about close family relationships and health, in a special issue of *American Psychologist* in September of 2017, examined the robust and indisputable association between close social relationships and health and well-being. In the introductory article of this special issue, UCLA psychology professor Christine Dunkel Schetter, PhD, writes that our health status is influenced by the effects of our close social relationships and the interactions associated with them. These interpersonal social connections affect our emotions, physiology, behavior, and cognition, and, ultimately, our health outcomes (Schetter, 2017, 511–516).

In "Advancing Social Connection as a Public Health Priority in the United States," which appears in the same issue, researchers Julianne Holt-Lunstad, PhD, Theodore Robles, PhD, and David Sbarra, PhD, conclude:

Humans need others to survive. Regardless of one's sex, country, or culture of origin, or age or economic background, social connection is crucial to human development, health, and survival. The evidence supporting this contention is unequivocal. When considering the umbrella term *social connection* and its constituent components, there are perhaps no other factors that can have such a large impact on both length and quality of life—from the cradle to the grave (p. 527).

In another article appearing in *American Psychologist* (September 2017), titled "Interpersonal Mechanisms Linking Close Relationships to Health," researchers Paula Pietromonaco, PhD, and Nancy Collins, PhD, draw a similar conclusion: "Close relationships can protect and promote health in various ways. In times of stress, relationships can buffer us from its negative effects, while in non-stressful times, relationships can foster positive emotions, personal growth, and health-promoting behaviors" (p. 533).

As the late Dr. Christopher Peterson, renowned psychologist and one of the founding fathers of the field of positive psychology, said, "There are no happy hermits."

Aging and Friendship

Researchers Karen Rook, PhD, and Susan Charles, PhD, studied social connections in older adulthood and observed that being socially involved is a predictor of better health across the life span and into older adult years. In the 2017 article, "Close Social Ties and Health in Later Life: Strengths and Vulnerabilities," published in *American Psychologist*, the researchers state:

Social relationships exert powerful influences on physical health in later adulthood, a critical consideration given age-related increases in the prevalence of chronic health conditions and physical disability. A large body of research indicates that older adults report greater satisfaction with their social networks than do younger adults, and that they often take measures to minimize their exposure to negative social encounters (p. 567).

In their article, Dr. Rook and Dr. Charles highlight emerging new studies (Schnettler & Wohler, 2015; Suanet, van Tilburg, & Broese van Groenou, 2013) that suggest that for older adults today, "non-kin ties" (or friends) offer more support than ever before in the U.S. as family structures and norms continue to change. For this age group, such social ties also play a key role in mitigating potential negative health outcomes resulting from relationship conflicts within social networks and/or the loss of one or more close friendships (Rook & Charles, 2017, 567–577).

William Chopik, PhD, assistant professor of psychology at Michigan State University, asserts (2017) that it is imperative to maintain healthy friendships: "Keeping a few really good friends around can make a world of difference for our health and well-being. So, it's smart to invest in the friendships that make you happiest." In his April 2017 article in the journal *Personal Relationships*, Dr. Chopik shares his findings from a pair of studies that involved nearly 280,000 people. He found that friendships become more essential to our health and happiness as we age. In addition, his research concluded that in older adults, friendships are a more robust predictor of our happiness and health than family member relationships. "Summaries of these studies," he writes, "show that friendships predict day-to-day happiness more [than other relationships] and ultimately how long we'll live, more so than spousal and family relationships" (Chopik, 2017, 408–422).

Cognition

Older adults who had strong social networks showed slower cognitive decline, according to another study, published in the October 2017 issue of the journal *PLOS One* by researchers at Northwestern University Feinberg School of Medicine. This study was the first to examine the social side of "SuperAgers"— those who are 80 years of age and older and demonstrate cognitive abilities that are at least as good as people in their fifties and sixties. These SuperAgers reported having more high-quality and satisfying relationships as compared to their cognitively average, same-age peers. Emily Rogalski, PhD, associate professor at Northwestern's Cognitive Neurology and Alzheimer's Disease Center, concluded, "You don't have to be the life of the party, but this study supports the theory that maintaining strong social networks seems to be linked to slower cognitive decline" (Northwestern University, 2017).

My friend Harriet is the perfect example of this principle—she just turned 90 years young! Although widowed a decade ago, she continues to live a vibrant, involved, and high-functioning life. She is active with her friends and family and still drives her car in her local area. This amazing lady also continues to travel internationally, and recently visited Africa where she participated in a safari. Over the years, I have had many conversations with her, and I find her fascinating and inspiring. She definitely qualifies as a "SuperAger" in every category. Quick-witted and cognitively sharp, she looks and acts much younger than most people 20 or 30 years her junior. What is her secret to the fountain of youth? Based on what I know about her, my theory is that she continues to connect with her circle of close friends and enjoys regular social events and outings with them. Her family jokes that you need to get on her calendar early; when they try to schedule a lunch or dinner with her, she has already booked dates with her friends. She is happy, healthy, and thriving, and she lives life to the fullest. This SuperAger could be our poster child for the theory that we are happiest and healthiest, and able to slow the cognitive aging process, when we stay in close connection with our circle of friends.

My Findings

In my work as a therapist, I have spoken with a handful of women who have confidently and proudly told me, "I don't have girlfriends, and I don't need them. Actually, I am just fine!" There are many reasons why people may make such statements. They might be in denial about their need for female friends; they may have been hurt by former friends and hesitant to take the risk again; or they may be trying to appear perfectly happy, independent, and self-sufficient. Regardless of the reason for their declaration about friendship, the bottom line is this: living life without female friends comes at a great expense. And it's an expense not only to your happiness level, but also to your overall quality of life.

An older client of mine provides a dramatic example of how connections with friends can turn around a physical and emotional decline. This 70-something-year-old woman had been living alone in her apartment for many years, not seeing people or getting out much. She was a widow and living a rather isolated existence, except for an appointment with her doctor's office or her visits to my office for our sessions. I observed that her cognition was declining rapidly as the months passed. It concerned me greatly, so I encouraged her to think about relocating to a retirement or assisted-living senior home, where she could enjoy fellowship with others her age and participate in events and organized meetups.

After much discussion and deliberation, she did move into a wonderful senior living retirement home and is thriving there today. After her move, I observed dramatic cognitive and emotional changes, and each time I saw her she looked happier and healthier. She was even more cognitively sharp in our sessions. When we discussed these positive changes, she explained to me that she loved having new friends to connect with at meals, and she enjoyed swapping life stories and attending movies and game nights together. This example poignantly illustrates what research tells us: we benefit from our friendship connections in a myriad of ways, especially as we age.

Here's what several women who responded to my questionnaire wrote about friendship:

- "Friendship is a very important facet of my life. Many times it keeps me sane. My friends are very therapeutic to me in good times and bad."
- "Friendship is the basis of my life. Without the female friendships I have experienced, my life would be hollow."
- "My friendships are an integral part of my physical, mental, and spiritual health. A true friend is there during the good and the bad."

I am reminded of the innate social bonds that promoted our ancestors' survival through the ages. Whether it was caring for the children, hunting for food, or fighting enemies, the group mentality prevailed and allowed our species to conquer challenges and survive. This deep need to bond and belong is an adaptive trait that has been passed on to us through the generations. We should not be surprised to learn we have been created and wired to be social. We are happiest, healthiest, and living our best lives when we honor this principle.

DISCUSSION QUESTIONS

1. Were you surprised with the research findings that age, gender, and income do not predict our happiness as much as having a network of close relationships? Explain how these findings may apply to your own life or the life of someone you know.

2. Can you remember a time when you were stressed and you were a recipient or practitioner of the "tend and befriend" solution to the stressful situation? Explain.

   a) How was this different from the way your husband or significant other dealt with a stressful situation?

3. Based on the research evidence presented in this chapter, how will your priorities change for spending time with girlfriends in the future?

   a) What new habits can you incorporate into your lifestyle to promote more time with girlfriends?

   b) What things seem to sabotage your girlfriend time and prevent it from happening? How can you change that pattern?

4. According to the 2010 BYU study, feeling disconnected from friends is twice as dangerous as obesity. Further, this study concluded that having connected friendships improves our odds of survival by 50 percent. Can you think of someone whom you may see as disconnected from social relationships?

   a) How might you talk to that person and share this research information to enlighten them about the merits of friendship for their health?

   b) How could you also partner with them to help them to become more social?

5. Is the research on friendships for older adults and the connection to health and happiness surprising to you?

   a) Give an example of an older adult whom you would characterize as living a full life and thriving with meaningful social connections.

   b) How could you encourage an older adult who is not as connected to begin to enjoy a more engaging social life?

   c) What are some ideas to employ in our own lives to stay socially connected, involved, and thriving as we become older adults?

6. According to the research study from Northwestern University, older adults who had strong social networks had slower cognitive decline. "SuperAgers" demonstrated cognitive abilities that were at least as strong as people 20 to 30 years younger than them. As a society, what can we do to encourage older adults to stay active and involved socially?

3

Paradigms for Perceiving Friendship

If your friendship is only for a season, then let it be for a full season.

William and Patricia Coleman,
Because We're Friends

UCLA psychology professor Christine Dunkel Schetter, PhD, offers that close relationships, such as those we see in our families and friendships, are defined by varying levels of interdependence. This interconnectivity is at the heart of women's friendships, and a wealth of great information is available that explains what female friendships look like and how they work (Dunkel Schetter, 2017, 511–516).

However, my own perspective on friendship seemed to call for a new paradigm—a novel framework to highlight my insights on this most relevant topic. The Olson Friendship Framework was born after much research, discussion, and analyzation of the history of real relationships. I will describe this innovative model for female friendship in detail, but first I'll explain why I developed it.

In researching practical friendship paradigms, I found only a few. Bestselling author Matthew Kelly covers the broader topic of relationships in what he terms "The Seven Levels of Intimacy," and he explains the importance of moving through them in our relationships as connection grows and becomes deeper and more intimate. He discusses how our friendships begin as casual and superficial, and they move through the intimacy levels as the degree of trust deepens through revealing hopes, dreams, feelings, fears, failures, faults, and needs (Kelly, 2005).

Shasta Nelson, MDiv, a strong advocate for female connection, portrays various "shades" of friendships in her "Circles of Connectedness Continuum." These are predicated on two primary factors: consistency and intimacy. Her paradigm is comprised of circles that represent five types of friendships, with categories ranging from the most casual to the most committed: *Contact Friends, Common Friends, Confirmed Friends, Community Friends,* and *Committed Friends.* Nelson maintains that these circles allow us to appreciate our current friendships as well as ascertain what types of relationships we still long to participate in (Nelson, 2013).

In *Grown-Up Girlfriends: Finding and Keeping Real Friends in the Real World,* therapists Erin Smalley and Carrie Oliver explain friendship levels using a basket analogy; for example, they call Basket One *Know-It-All Friends,* and it is made up of those girlfriends you consider friends of the heart and soul. These relationships have a higher level of trust and commitment, are intimate, and require the most time. Friends in Basket Two, *Good Friends or Companions,* are those with whom you share common hobbies, activities, and concerns, as well as some parallel perspectives. Basket Three, *Acquaintances*, is the least intimate. These relationships are very casual and superficial, and include those friends you see in public places, such as stores and offices, during your daily routines (Smalley & Oliver, 2007).

The Olson Friendship Framework

But the question remains: What influences affect these connections? Why are some friendships destined to become best friends while others remain acquaintances for decades?

While each of these paradigms is a useful tool for explaining the complexity of friendships, I feel there is a need for a clear and simple model to help you visualize the interdependence of the following levels of friendship:

1. Acquaintances
2. Outer Circle Friends
3. Casual Friends
4. Inner Circle Friends
5. Best Friends

Each level has its own attributes, while also encompassing those of the circle or circles outside of it. The largest circle is on the outside (*Acquaintances*), and the nested circles continue to shrink as you move toward the smallest circle in the center (*Best Friends*). We are the most invested in this tiny circle because it is our most intimate and deepest point of friendship connection.

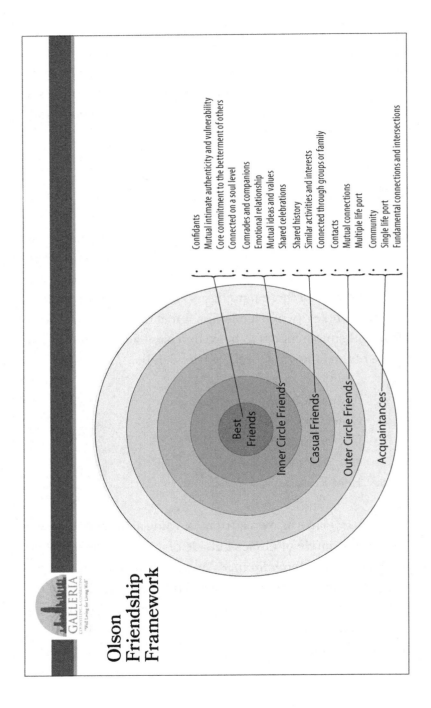

Olson
Friendship
Framework

GALLERIA
COGNITIVE & CONSULTING
"Well Living for Living Well"

Best Friends

Inner Circle Friends

Casual Friends

Outer Circle Friends

Acquaintances

Confidants
Mutual intimate authenticity and vulnerability
Core commitment to the betterment of others
Connected on a soul level

Comrades and companions
Emotional relationship
Mutual ideas and values
Shared celebrations

Shared history
Similar activities and interests
Connected through groups or family

Contacts
Mutual connections
Multiple life port

Community
Single life port
Fundamental connections and intersections

Friendship Attributes

Friendship Attributes	Best Friend	Inner Circle	Casual Friend	Outer Circle	Acquaintance
Confidant	•				
Mutual intimate authenticity and vulnerability	•				
Core commitment to the betterment of other	•				
Connected on a soul level	•				
Comrade and companion	•	•			
Emotional relationship	•	•			
Mutual ideals and values	•	•			
Shared celebrations	•	•			
Shared history	•	•	•		
Similar activities and interests	•	•	•		
Connected through groups or family	•	•	•		
Contact	•	•	•	•	
Mutual connections	•	•	•	•	
Multiple life port	•	•	•	•	
Community	•	•	•	•	•
Single life port	•	•	•	•	•
Fundamental connections and intersections	•				•

Levels of Friendship

Let's examine each of the five levels of friendship in detail to understand the traits and characteristics that give that level its distinctive flavor and parameters. We will begin with the outermost circle, *Acquaintances*, and work toward the inner, core circle of *Best Friends*.

Level 1 Acquaintances

The outer circle, *Acquaintances*, is the largest and is made up of all of our associates, with whom we share the most fundamental connection or intersection in life. For instance, this might be a person we know from our church, community, coffee shop, gym, yoga class, or our child's school, someone we see only at that place; we only know them in that setting and do not share a connection outside of it.

Reasonable Expectations of Acquaintances

- Sharing a common activity together
- Enjoying lighthearted conversations
- Exchanging superficial stories, facts, and pleasantries

Level 2 Outer Circle Friends

The next circle is *Outer Circle Friends*, which includes the people you share multiple life ports or connections with. This may be a neighbor who also works out at the same gym. You see her in different settings and share several common paths, but you do not share much outside of those settings.

This category of friendship can include a lot of different people whom you see frequently and in these common settings.

Reasonable Expectations of Outer Circle Friends

- Having common goals and ideas
- Connecting through social or neighborhood events
- Enjoying a positive, pleasant, superficial relationship

Level 3 Casual Friends

The next level refers to people with whom we share a common history, interests, and activities. *Casual Friends* also consist of those we are connected to through family functions or groups; examples include parents of our children's friends with whom we have shared many functions over the years at soccer games, birthday parties, church activities, and holiday gatherings. Someone who is in our book club, but who is also a neighbor and a fellow member of our dinner club group, falls into this category. We enjoy spending time in a casual way with these friends and participating in common interests and events together, but they are not at the level of a deep emotional friendship, nor are they people we would confide in or seek to share with at a difficult time in our lives.

Reasonable Expectations of Casual Friends

- Spending special events together: holidays, celebrations, club parties, sports activities, church gatherings, etc.
- Sharing memories of a common history together
- Connecting through reciprocal support for each other
- Enjoying mutual fellowship and companionship

Level 4 Inner Circle Friends

Inner Circle Friends are defined by a close relationship that is based on mutual ideals, values, and communal celebrations. These friends are seen as comrades and companions who we consider to be deserving of our trust and confidence. This connection results in an emotional relationship that feels safe and secure. We feel a special connection to these people that is predicated on the principles that we all embrace and try to live by.

Reasonable Expectations of Inner Circle Friends

- Discussing each other's fears, feelings, and faults
- Trusting in a confidential connection that is safe and secure
- Expecting a deep and unwavering loyalty
- Celebrating each other's successes, joys, and victories
- Supporting one another during challenges and struggles

Level 5 Best Friends

The fifth and most inner circle is the *Best Friends* level of friendship. This level exists as a bond that is rich, deep, and resistant to life challenges. The heartbeat sustaining this bond is unique to the relationship, connecting the souls in an intimate and personal way.

Best friends are defined, of course, by all of the traits of the four outer circles, plus the most intimate qualities of this core level. Most of us only have a handful of friends who will meet these criteria at any one time in our lives, or even throughout our life span. The intimate qualities in this fifth level include core connection to the betterment of the others, mutual authenticity and vulnerability, heart-to-heart connections, and being confidants.

Our most trusted confidants know our deepest secrets, and it is highly likely that we also know many of theirs. This type of friendship has a natural flow, a back-and-forth of sharing and caring. As soul mates, these people truly "get us" and vice versa. We help support and facilitate each other in our respective journeys to be the best we can be. Sometimes this may mean we have to be brutally honest or challenge our friend to stop engaging in a self-sabotaging behavior. Or they may need to be the ones who challenge us and point out our destructive patterns. But the essential point is that the friendship is strong and deep enough to withstand these criticisms. In fact, because the relationship is built on a mutual trust and authenticity, this objective viewpoint (criticism) serves to only strengthen the bond of the friendship. We are willing to be raw with each other because we feel secure and accepted. We are truly ourselves in these relationships, willing to risk being vulnerable and exposing our "soft spots."

Reasonable Expectations of Best Friends

- Exposing our souls so that we may be free to be completely authentic and vulnerable
- Challenging each other to be the best version of ourselves
- Connecting as confidants in a climate of non-judgmental trust
- Relating on the deepest level of emotional intimacy

The Olson Friendship Framework highlights the different traits and dynamics that define the five levels of friendships. This framework makes clear that the connections shared between friends is distinct, and those connections vary depending on the level of the circle defining the relationship. For instance, *Casual Friends* may enjoy a shared history, and participating in similar activities together, but they fall short of the soul level connection that those in the innermost circle enjoy, those who are *Best Friends*.

About the Levels of Friendship

Before going any further on the levels of friendship, I must mention what could be a common misunderstanding: All levels of friendship have worth and value. It would be a mistake to assume that a friendship that is not at the Inner Circle or Best Friends level is a less-valuable or less-important relationship. People play different roles in our lives, and thus our connection to them is unique and important for what that friendship offers to us and what we offer to the other person. It would not be realistic to think that all our connections could be at the soul-mate level, or even at the Inner Circle level. But everyone plays an important part in our life's tapestry. Our lives are made richer and more colorful by the connection we share with them.

Let me give you an example of this from my own life journey. I became friends many years ago with someone in my profession. She has been a wonderful friend through the years, and although I do not see her on a regular basis, we continue to enjoy reaching out to each other through cell phone and social media. When we can plan a lunch date or a girlfriend meetup, we both enjoy it and pick up where we left off. I would consider her a Casual Friend, but our friendship is still very special, meaningful, and important to both of us! We continue this friendship because it is pleasurable, and we find it rewarding and joyful at its current level.

Friendship Fluidity

Since many factors affect how people come and go in our lives, there are no easy ways to predict who will be a forever friend and who will always remain an Outer Circle Friend. It is possible for people to begin their friendship at the Acquaintances level, but then move quickly through the circles to become Best Friends in record time due to life circumstances. And it is just as possible for people to spend decades being friends at only the Casual Friends level, never moving beyond that circle to a deeper and more connected friendship level. There are so many aspects at play here that predicting with certainty which friendships will move up to Best Friends status is nearly impossible.

Friendship and Life Cycles

Many people have reported being in female friendships that, although fun, meaningful, and rewarding, only lasted a few years. Suddenly, and for no apparent reason, that friendship slipped away. When this happens, we try to make sense of it, but nothing seems especially obvious.

Our relationships are affected by our lives and what is going on with us as we move through our life chapters. We are all well aware that nothing stays the same for long, and for most of us, just as we become comfortable with a routine or a "known" in our world, it changes! And in many cases, our "life changes" trickle down to our friendships.

There is a saying that "Friends come into our lives for a reason or a season." Sometimes the friendship we are in begins to change due to a move to a new city or state, or a life change that makes our connection to that person strained or different in terms of time or distance. Over the years, many of my female clients have shared their personal stories about the friendships that they enjoyed with other moms from their children's activities or school. One client recalled how she was hurt and disappointed when she realized that her special friendships with other moms were changing and becoming more distant because their children no longer shared the same activities. It was difficult for her to come to the realization that these friends were in her life for a season, but now the season was over, and it was time to move on and celebrate the friendship for the part it had played in her life.

As we look in the rearview mirror and re-examine the many friendships that have come and gone in life, as well as those that are still present, we see many common patterns in our female friendships. In my recent research with all ages of women, I concluded that these types of patterns are universal to all of us. In some cases, we still enjoy vibrant relationships with longtime friends who have been in our circle for decades. In other cases, we are no longer connected to wonderful girlfriends we shared great times with due to geography or life transitions.

Perceptions in Friendship

As psychotherapists like to say, "Our perception is our reality." We see this play out clearly in examining the dynamics of friendship. One of the pitfalls that can trip us up results when our perception of the friendship level is different than our friend's perception. When it becomes apparent, this can result in hurt feelings, disappointment, and even anger. I call these mismatched perceptions in friendship levels *danger zones*. They usually arise when the friends perceive their relationship as two or more levels apart. Since we all bring a different set of ideas and expectations to our friendships based on our unique backgrounds, life histories, needs, biases, and personalities, it is entirely possible that one person's view of the friendship will be very different from the other person's, creating a vastly different picture of expectations.

For instance, one girlfriend may see her friend as a Casual Friend while the other may, in turn, consider her a Best Friend. These two types of friendships are two levels apart, and thus they typically operate much differently. This disconnect in how these two girlfriends perceive their bond can sometimes lead to hurt feelings, conflict, disappointment, confusion, and could potentially lead to the demise of the relationship. If the friends are able to openly discuss their difference in perceptions of the friendship, however, it is possible they may be able to keep the friendship after making adjustments and clarifying their expectations of each other and the relationship.

In my weekend seminar for women called "The Healing Power of Girlfriends," I ask participants to do an important exercise to demonstrate how perceptions can play a part in the course of friendships. They are given two handouts: (a) "How You Perceive Others See You" and (b) "How You See Others." I ask participants to carefully consider their answers as they fill these out. (If you are interested in viewing these two handouts, they are on my website at http:// GalleriaCounseling.com.)

For "How You Perceive Others See You," the participants are asked to imagine how their friends would categorize them; in other words, they are invited to consider which level of the friendship circle that a friend would assign to their friendship. For "How You See Others," each participant is instructed to place their friends in one of the five circles according to her own perception of the friendship.

Once all forms are complete, we discuss the "so what" of this drill: "Do your friends put you at the same level as you put them?" This exercise highlights for us the different *expectations* in friendships.

People struggle with these situations and often end up feeling depressed and sad when friendships seem difficult or hard to understand. We all begin to play the "blame game" and try to point a finger at what could have caused the problems. We start the "woulda-coulda-shoulda" game. We second-guess ourselves and think about how we might have tried harder to be a better friend, or we come up with reasons why this person does not think of us as a "bestie."

We are best served by accepting the friendship as it is, and just letting time and life happen. If this friendship is meant to become more connected and richer, it will naturally flow and develop. Our journey in life has a way of sorting it all out.

Over the years, I have come to learn patience with this process. There have been many times that I wanted to rush the friendship—to get to that BFF level because I really liked a new friend and felt such a strong connection to her. However, a friendship is much like a good wine. You have to give it time to mature and age properly, and the process cannot be rushed or the end quality is compromised. Allowing the friendship to ripen and become enriched from life circumstances gives it a depth that cannot be matched.

If the friendship stays at an outer level and there is no movement toward a deeper, best friend-kind of relationship, it is important for us to accept this for what it is and not feel guilty or try to overthink it too much. We are wise to focus on the positives of what that friendship means to us and celebrate the part it plays in our life journey. We will be much happier and emotionally healthy if we can adopt this approach instead of ruminating about the disappointments and the feelings of loss and grief.

Dimensions of Friendship Expectations

Another way to conceptualize the levels of friendships is to define the relationship according to the Dimensions of Friendship Expectations. This design approaches friendship relationships from a practical approach, describing and clustering expectations that could exist on each level of the Olson Friendship Framework. It views the concept of friendship from a real-life slant; in other words, what does friendship look like when we get into the trenches? What happens when people have emergencies and need help, or lose a spouse and need love and emotional support?

Here are the clusters of friendship expectations that spring from the levels of intimacy in the Olson Friendship Framework and how those tie into real-life situations. I have divided these into three categories:

- Time, Talent, and Treasures
- Reason or Season
- Share and Care

Each category spotlights a unique and specific set of values and characteristics for that flavor of friendship. This helps us view our girlfriend relationships along dimensions that give us perspective on the purpose, parameters, and mechanics of the friendship.

Let's look at these one at a time and explore each in more detail.

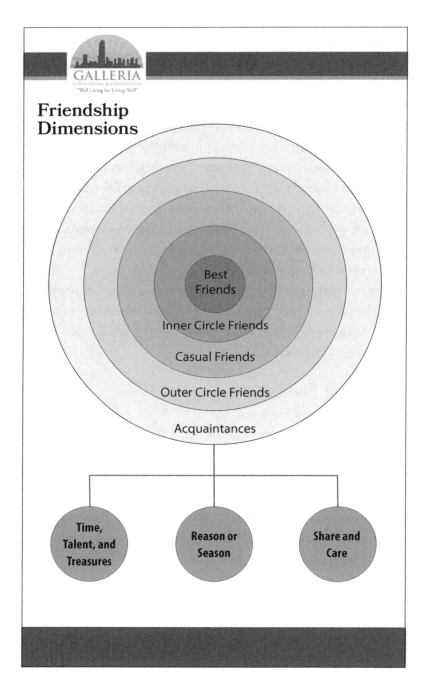

Time, Talent, and Treasures

This category is defined by a system of give-and-take and involves a notion of reciprocal back-and-forth between friends. We give to others as they have needs, and others give to us as we have needs. We share our time, our talents, and our treasures with each other. In this dimension, there is an unspoken understanding: if I am having a struggle or difficulty, my friend will jump right in to offer help and support, quite possibly without me even needing to ask. I will, likewise, do this for her when she needs assistance. Typically, we see this sharing of time, talents, and treasures more prominently in the deeper level of friendships as we connect and share more of each other's lives. However, it is also totally possible that a more casual outer circle friend would share her resources to help a friend in need.

I have actually witnessed this happen where more casual friends or acquaintances have participated in acts of kindness to support or encourage a friend in need. In 2017, Hurricane Harvey devastated our hometown of Houston and left millions of people affected by the flood waters in the aftermath. We saw powerful examples of the innate good in humanity as neighbors or strangers came together to help each other, even while sometimes putting their own lives at risk. It provides a poignant snapshot of how connected we are as humans and just how profound it is when people share their time, talents, and treasures with others, with no expectation of anything in return.

Reason or Season

In the next category, we may enjoy a friendship that is based on a reason—a shared activity or purpose—or a season—a specific period of time or a chapter in our lives. In the first, we engage in the relationship because it is centered on a mutual purpose or goal. Depending on the people and circumstances involved, some of these friendships continue and thrive for years, while others may end completely once the shared purpose or goal is completed or is no longer relevant.

Season relationships are centered on a mutual sharing of a particular time period or season of life. The shared journey during this chapter of life creates a sense of closeness and connectedness. Often, once this chapter is complete and the season is over, the friendship may change and become more distant, or possibly even end. But the value of the connection during this time period is no less important, even if the friendship does not last after the season is completed. What is essential is to find a way to reframe this friendship so that we value it for the part it played in our life story, even though the season is now over. Human nature is such that we will often try to put this friendship-for-a-season into a negative box of memories because it ended. In reality, it would be more beneficial to reframe this as an important part of our journey and celebrate what this friendship gave to us. It is essential to value our female relationships for the unique dynamic they contributed, and not to detract from their significance because the friendship did not last.

Friends for a Season

When we lived in Milwaukee and I was pregnant with our third child, I met five other pregnant moms in a prenatal exercise class. These new friends became my new support group as we all related to the challenges of pregnancy, life with little ones already in our nests, and being stay-at-home moms. Our pregnancies progressed as we continued in our weekly exercise class, and so did our friendships. We were all due within days of each other, which was pretty amazing in the grand scheme of things.

We would often go out to lunch after our class and watch people's heads turn when the six of us very pregnant ladies entered the restaurant. One by one, we each had our babies as our delivery dates arrived. Afterward, we all met up for our own postpartum support group, which was hosted at a different house each week. These women were my lifeline to sanity, and I look back now and am grateful for those trusted connections that gave so much support, encouragement, validation, humor, and most importantly, sisterhood, during a challenging time in my life as a young mom with two preschoolers and a new baby. Although these friendships changed when I moved to Texas, they remain strong in my life story as "Friends for a Season," and I treasure each of those connections for the part they played in my journey.

Share and Care

The third category is defined by a depth and understanding at its core, and operates at the pinnacle, so to speak, of our friendship levels. In this dimension, there is a strong commitment to the friendship and to each other, as well as shared authenticity as mutual confidants, which emphasizes a high degree of trust, respect, and shared values. Such friends bare their souls and allow the raw parts of themselves to float to the surface in the safety and comfort of this profound level of friendship. We may only ever know a handful of people who qualify for this category, as these types of connections present themselves to us less frequently. More resilient than less-intimate levels of friendship, the bonds in these relationships are powerful, resistant to life's ups and downs, and mutually valued by the two friends.

The other part of this Share and Care concept of friendship is to perceive the relationship in terms of how we support and show love and caring for each other. During times of life's trials and tribulations, we often see our friends jump into action. This is so validating and confirms to us how committed they are to our well-being and our friendship. Whether through mourning the loss of a loved one by bringing in food or flowers, offering to help pick our kids up from school after we have been in the hospital, or just being a shoulder to cry on, it means the world to not feel alone in a time of need and grief. Sharing and caring is one way we can live out our love in real ways and in real time.

Treasured Examples of Sharing and Caring

My wonderful friend Pat showed this gift of sharing and caring in a very special way. Many years ago, while I was in graduate school, she offered to pick up my kids from middle school since she was already picking her own up. She insisted on helping me out because I was driving 90 minutes each way—every day—to the university. As we discussed these arrangements, I could not believe her kindness and her selfless desire to ease my load by taking one more worry off my over-flowing plate. She was my angel, and her sharing and caring kept me sane that year, to say the least! I will forever be grateful for this treasured friend, whose actions continue to show her love and support for others every day.

Lisa, a dear neighbor-friend, touched my soul in ways I will never forget during Hurricane Harvey in August, 2017.

I was in Mexico with friends, when all flights home to Houston were canceled. At the same time, my husband was working 24/7 with all the first responders to provide emergency medical care. This left my two senior cats, who were in delicate health to ride out the storm alone. So I called Lisa, who offered to feed and care for them; she found Chloe, our beautiful calico cat, lethargic and sickly.

Lisa provided TLC and sent me a precious video she took of Chloe. Sadly, Chloe crossed the rainbow bridge a few days later, before I arrived home. Although this left me with a giant hole in my heart, my dear friend Lisa had given both Chloe and me indescribable gifts. Yes, there are angels among us, and they are called girlfriends!

Applying the Olson Friendship Framework in Your Life

It is helpful to explore the different dimensions of friendships and spend time pondering these various levels of relationships and what they mean to us. In understanding the framework of different friendship designs, we can come to appreciate each level for what it is and what part it plays in our life journey. Not all friendships are created equal, nor should they be. By having a more clear and comprehensive understanding of how friendships operate, we can then participate in them more fully and with informed purpose.

I've presented a lot of information and concepts to facilitate our understanding of female friendships in this chapter. The Olson Friendship Framework was designed to provide a visual paradigm as a tool to educate and explain the various levels of intimacy in female relationships. Perhaps you've found yourself in situations where you've been confused, disappointed, frustrated, blindsided, or shocked by the action of a person you considered a friend or trusted confidant. With this new framework, you now have a clearer lens for expectations and limitations. Going forward, you'll be better equipped with more accurate knowledge of the intricacies and implications in friendships with your women friends. The ultimate goal is to be more empowered in how we participate in our female relationships to ensure we can maximize our enjoyment and minimize our disappointment.

DISCUSSION QUESTIONS

1. Think of a time in your life when your friendship with a girlfriend ended and left you feeling confused and perplexed. Looking back on that today, how might you apply some of the concepts you have learned in this chapter to understanding this relationship within a new friendship framework? Explain and discuss.

2. After looking at the Olson Friendship Framework and the levels of friendship, think of some friends who have moved in and out of your circles due to life transitions and changes. What are some of the life lessons you have learned from these experiences with friendships?

3. Think of a relationship in which you put a friend in a deeper level of friendship than they assigned to you.

    a) What level would they assign to you on the Olson Friendship Framework? What level would you ascribe to them?

    b) How did this cause problems for the relationship?

    c) How has the friendship survived this challenge? Explain.

4. We tend to enter the "danger zone" when the friendship is two or more levels apart based on our perceptions as compared to our girlfriend's. When was a time you found yourself in this danger zone, and how did you navigate through this?

5. Using the Dimensions of Friendship Expectations is another way to conceive of the connections in our girl-friend relationships. How have you participated in the Time, Talents, and Treasures back-and-forth, give-and-take friendship connection with your friends?

   a) What are some ways your friendships became more meaningful, more connected, and more intimate from sharing this concept of Time, Talents, and Treasures?

   b) It is the reciprocal back-and-forth quality of this that makes these friendships work. But there are times when the reciprocal part is missing, and only you are giving and caring in the friendship. If you've had this experience, how did you deal with this issue, and how did it affect your friendship?

6. The dimension called Reason or Season is a way to conceive of friendship. Think of a friend or friends who came into your life for a specific reason or during a particular season.

   a) How did those people play a special part in your life journey?

   b) How were you changed by that friendship at that time and in your current friendships?

7. The dimension of friendship called Share and Care represents the pinnacle of a core female friendship. We share and care on a deep level and enjoy an authentic and intimate connection based on trust and honesty. Think of a time when you have participated in this kind of a special bond in friendship with a current girlfriend.

a) How do you and your friend show your support and encouragement for each other? How do you show signs of caring and love to each other?

b) How does this bond in your friendship spill over into other parts of your life and color your worldview of female friendships?

4

The Anatomy of Friendships

My friends have made the story of my life. In a thousand ways, they
have turned my limitations into beautiful privileges.

Helen Keller

In this chapter, we will explore some of the core components of the friendship relationship structure, including
boundaries, personalities, power, and friendship histories. Through a more in-depth understanding of the anatomy
of these relationships, we can gain a more comprehensive
appreciation for all the dynamics at play.

Boundaries

I have spent countless hours in sessions with my female clients
discussing relationship issues that center around boundaries.
To be in healthy relationships, we need to honor each other's
individuality, autonomy, space, and limits. These are the key
ingredients that comprise boundaries.

Boundaries are an outcome of our own sense of self, and they work to put limits where they are needed. We are healthiest and happiest in relationships when we understand ourselves, have a strong sense of identity, and respect ourselves and our boundaries. Boundaries allow us to function safely and securely in our relationships so that we honor our limits while still fully participating in our friendships. For example, it is imperative that we do not make our happiness conditional on our friends' happiness because this sets us up for disappointment and boundary issues.

How to Establish Healthy Boundaries in a Friendship

Sometimes we may find ourselves in friendships where we feel we have been manipulated, disrespected, or on the receiving end of broken trust. These are all boundary issues, and they need to be addressed in the friendship.

How do we establish boundaries in our friendships? The simple answer is through honest and helpful dialogue between friends. If you can reach resolution by straight talk with a friend, the boundary issue can be put on the table and discussed. Friends who value the relationship will usually want to make the adjustments and work on the boundary problems to preserve the friendship. In these situations, the friendship will emerge healthier and stronger than before. However, it is possible that discussion of these boundary violations will not be embraced and could potentially lead to conflict and termination of the relationship.

I worked with one client who was in a friendship that became problematic and rather toxic. She found herself on the receiving end of numerous trust issues, where confidential information, which was extremely private and was only meant to stay between the two of them, was shared with others. My client was devastated when she learned that her trusted friend had actually spoken to others about this private information. In addition, issues of manipulation and lack of respect also came to play in their friendship soon after, which caused further heartbreak and frustration.

One of my mantras with my clients is to always "pay attention to patterns." In retrospect, it was easy to see how this friendship failed the boundary test and was not healthy on any level. As my client and I evaluated the real "bones" of this friendship, it became clear that there was not much there to salvage. The healthiest solution for my client was to give this so-called friendship its wings and let it go. In processing the dynamics of this female friendship, my client was able to see a distinct pattern of how her friend had not respected healthy boundaries throughout the years of the friendship.

Another example of a friendship where boundaries were not honored is a story of a young stay-at-home mom who was repeatedly "dumped" on by a friend of hers for childcare needs when the mom who had a job outside of the house had to work late. This type of boundary issue usually begins quite innocently with a "favor" to help out a friend in need, and then becomes a pattern of boundary issues where one friend feels taken advantage of by the other.

This calls for a "Hey! Time out! Let's Chat!" moment where honest and open feelings can be shared. If you feel taken advantage of in a relationship, then speak up. We need to honor our own boundaries and feelings in our friendships for them to be healthy. If we allow the pattern to continue, we only feel abused and demeaned in the friendship. By addressing the issue, the pattern can change and new healthy behaviors can emerge. If the friendship is stable, both people can move forward after making these adjustments to participate in an improved and richer friendship. Friendships operate much like other issues in our everyday lives: we see a need for change, we tweak things a bit, and we move on to higher ground.

The bottom line is this: there are lots of potential friends out there in the world for us to discover, and we do not have to settle for unhealthy friendships where unhealthy boundaries define the relationship.

Personalities

Our female friendships are influenced by our personalities and how our traits mesh together. The flow of friendship is a sort of rhythm that is created by the personality style of each person as they come together and interact. When two women become friends, the relationship they share is not equal to the sum of their individual parts.

The blending of personalities adds texture and definition to the friendship. I know my life has been greatly blessed and colored by the many women I have shared a friendship with. My girlfriends' different personality styles bring out a different side of me, too. The benefit of this is that I have been able to grow in my friendships and grow personally as a woman.

As I recall these connections through the various chapters of my life, I realize that each unique person and friendship has shaped the outlines of my soul and touched the spirit within forever. The beautiful part of aging is that you can see how you have grown and evolved within the friendship, or at times, even because of it. Looking back now over friendships that started in my twenties, thirties, forties, and fifties, I clearly see how those unique connections have shaped the person I am today. I am grateful for each special friendship and each unique personality that has supplied a piece of the colorful path that makes up my cumulative story.

Introverts and Extroverts

One of the biggest debates about personality and friendship revolves around the question of who makes better friends—introverts or extroverts. The answer is . . . *both*. They each have unique qualities and vibes. In the end, it does not matter if you are a pedigreed extrovert or introvert, or maybe a hybrid. No matter how we self-identify, we need the same things from our friendships, and we share more common ground than we are probably even aware.

Most of us tend to have a certain level of comfort with particular personality types. My own personality leans more toward extroversion, but I equally enjoy wonderful and meaningful friendships with both extroverts and introverts. Each friendship creates its own special and unique dynamic, and that is what makes the relationship so very valuable and precious.

Respecting how we are different and how that may also determine our needs for socialization in friendships is critical. Introverts may prefer to share time in more quiet and intimate settings, while our extroverted friends may enjoy bigger groups with more activity and energy.

Whether you are someone who prefers just hanging out with one or two close friends for the evening or you love a Friday night social with fifteen of your closest and dearest buddies, we all want the same things in the end. We want to feel validated by our friends and would like to have a chance to share our story, talk about our lives, and be heard and understood. We just want to be with people who truly care and who "get" us.

In the end, our personality styles serve to lend color and shape to any friendship, and they enrich the flavor of the relationship in unique ways. Let me share a couple examples in my own circle of friends to highlight this point.

We know that humor is healing, and laughing with our friends is an easy way to inject some humor into our stressful lives when we feel emotionally exhausted. I share a long friendship with a girlfriend who has an endearing sense of humor. Her gift of comedy brings a certain lightness and energy to our friendship that turns my ordinary day into an extraordinary one. After we hang up from our chats, I often find myself chuckling as I go about my day thinking about a funny quip or a silly story she shared. It's truly difficult to have a bad day after chatting with her. If you are a friend who has been blessed with this gift of humor, I encourage you to share it often with friends who will benefit.

Another example of personality styles adding a richness or texture to friendships would be what I experience with my three Ya-Ya girlfriends. We all have different personalities for sure, ranging from introverted to extroverted to a combination of both. Even though we aren't able to come together often because we live in three different states, our personality styles add color and sparkle to our gatherings. We share humor, thoughtfulness, attentive listening, and acts of kindness, and we affirm and encourage each other. Each one of us brings a different gift to the table of friendship that enriches and embellishes the collective whole of our Ya-Ya sisterhood.

Being able to accept each other with our individual personality traits, whether we are wired to be introverted or extroverted, is key to having healthy and happy friendships. Planning our time with friends and honoring how they are most comfortable socializing with us is imperative to the ongoing success of and satisfaction with the friendship.

Power

Different styles of the power structure are at play in any relationship, whether it's a business partnership or a marriage, and our female friendships are not much different. Power, a dynamic construct that changes across time and situations, often determines the course of the relationship. How we are with power in our girlfriend friendships can sometimes make or break the relationship.

Typically, we see people most satisfied when the power is shared and there is mostly equal input from both parties. Women who have been in friendships where the power structure was fairly one-sided tend to come to the same conclusions: they feel that although unequal power may work in the early stages of the friendship, eventually they tire of not having a voice in the decisions, agendas, or schedules of day-to-day life. If this becomes a pattern over time, it can cause issues and decrease the satisfaction of participating in the friendship. In some cases, unless things can be resolved and changed, it may result in the friendship ending.

Through my decades of working as a therapist with women, I have heard many stories in which power became a stumbling block for the survival of the relationship. In some situations, these women were able to help their friends understand how unfair the power was playing out, and these friendships continued and were healthier once power was shared more equally. In other cases, the friendships did not last because the power struggles continued to cause conflicts and power behaviors did not change.

As we know, most friendships flow best when there is reciprocal energy. The concept of power in the relationship works in a similar fashion, and in most friendships, there is a harmony or synergy created when both people share the power. From decisions like where to go for lunch to who will drive the carpool to the kids' soccer practices, we all like to have our ideas or wishes acknowledged and honored.

One of my clients struggled in a friendship with a lady who had a very strong personality and was controlling. This friend maintained a lot of power in the relationship and took on a role in the friendship that was like a parent to a child. My client became weary of always being on the receiving end of instructions from her friend, never really getting a chance for any input or decision making. We worked on how she could find her voice in the friendship and begin to assert her own opinions and preferences. She did this by first being honest and open with her friend about feeling controlled in their relationship. While my client acknowledged her friend's great ideas about where to go, have lunch, shop, etc., she also expressed a desire participate in making decisions about their activities in an equal and fair manner. By becoming more assertive and vocal in the friendship, she was able to successfully alter the power structure and boundaries in the friendship and maintain the relationship, although with new parameters.

It is part of the human spirit to want to feel validated and heard by others. We are most satisfied and happy in our relationships when others value us, and we, in turn, value them. Splitting the power in the friendship is one way we can accomplish mutual respect.

Friendship Histories

When we begin a new friendship, we bring with us the histories of our old friendships. This includes our wounds, expectations, disappointments, successes, joys, vulnerabilities, and frames of reference. Our life experiences create a template for friendship, and this definitely has an impact on how we move forward into new friendships.

I once worked with a client who had been in many friendships where she'd felt betrayed, disrespected, and not valued as a trusted confidant. Friendship histories created negative thoughts of pain and sadness for her, and to move forward into new friendships and be able to find a place of loyalty, honor, and respect was a major challenge. Her friendship histories had left her with a jaded view of female relationships, and they created a sea of doubt in her mind that healthy friendships even existed. Our goals included helping her develop tools to assess what traits to look for and what to avoid in new potential friendships. After much hard work examining her friendship history, and then developing strategies for moving forward, she was eventually able to trust again and enjoy new female friendships built on the framework of respect and loyalty.

Tips for Avoiding Unhealthy New Friendships

These are four of the essential things to remember when scouting for new friendships.

1. **Keep Your Eyes Open.** Be observant of how new potential girlfriends talk about, treat, and interact with their friends. If they appear to be gossipers, backstabbers, or two-faced about their other female friends, you could be next. Instead, look for girlfriends who seem honest, genuine, kind, giving, nonjudgmental, and respectful.

2. **Drama Queens Are Not Welcome.** If these new friends seem to like drama and are always in the middle of a new soap opera, beware! This could be the "play" you are signing up to be a part of if you continue the relationship.

3. **Check Neediness at the Friendship Door.** Do these new friends seem to have a high degree of neediness? Do they require lots of emotional support and ask you to be giving all the time? If so, then evaluate if this is a friendship you will enjoy and benefit from emotionally.

4. **Antennas Up for Toxic Friends.** Be careful when encountering people who display negative behaviors of competition, anger, envy, revenge, rage, criticism, and narcissism. These behaviors are the ingredients for a toxic relationship. Being able to spot these traits in friends takes a little practice, but it is well worth honing your skills to do so. It will save you heartache and pain down the road. For example, be wary if your friend always displays competitive behaviors with you, or she struggles to be genuinely happy for you when things go your way and you enjoy success. True friends don't behave this way.

Friendship histories also may include joy and happiness as we recall the good times shared and the memories made with girlfriends. My work with clients, as well as participating in my own female friendships, has given me a wide lens in which to assess the anatomy of these relationships. As we look back and remember the times shared, hopefully we will have many more positive memories than negative ones. I can honestly say that over the decades there have been many more cherished and beloved friendships that enriched my life and fed my soul than those that led to disappointment.

When Friendships End

Not all friendships work out, though. Not all people turn out to be true friends, so we all have histories that include those relationships as well. Some people have been in friendships that have been hurtful or ended abruptly for no clear reason. In therapy sessions, my clients and I will discuss some of the possible culprits that may have played a part in the demise of the friendship. One of my clients shared her story of a valued friendship that did not last more than a few years, as her friend became quite competitive with her. She soon realized her friend was growing distant, and this spirit of competition started to interfere with their friendship connection. This led to a breakdown in communication, and it ultimately impacted their close and intimate friendship as well. My client was saddened to see this change in their connection, which had once been such a wonderful shared source of joy and camaraderie.

Focusing on the ways in which our lives have been enhanced by true friendships is much more productive than emphasizing the times we were disappointed or hurt along the way. We do need to be realistic and aware that sometimes—for whatever reason—a friendship may not last. The good news is we can always reframe things and remember that although a friendship may have been cut short, we played a part in their life journey, and they played a part in ours.

Of course, sometimes we also just need to give ourselves permission to take some time and mourn the loss of the friendship as we make adjustments and move on. It is helpful for some people to reframe this loss and disappointment and focus on the positive parts that came out of the relationship. In other words, we try to look at the good things that we learned about ourselves, the fun times when we laughed together, or the enduring benefits the friendship has left us with today. The bottom line is this: we need to believe in ourselves and believe that we still have something valuable to offer to others, and then get up and get back in the game. What is essential is to find a way to reframe the failed friendship so it does not wipe out the many deep and special core friendships we treasure and hold dear.

Boundaries, personalities, power, and histories all play their part in the development of the bond that connects two people. Having an awareness of these factors can allow us to better navigate the waters in friendship and deal with the swirling rapids that we sometimes find ourselves in.

DISCUSSION QUESTIONS

1. Think of a time in a friendship when you experienced issues with boundaries. Discuss this situation and how you addressed the problems with your friend.

   a) Were you able to resolve the boundary issues, and if so, how was the friendship affected?

   b) Manipulation can play a part in boundary issues. Discuss a time when manipulation was a factor in a boundary situation in your friendship.

2. As you look back over your female friendships, how have those friends' different personality types shaped your personality?

   a) Do you tend to be more extroverted or introverted in your personality style?

   b) How does this affect the personality types you tend to usually gravitate toward?

3. When did power become an issue in a friendship? How did you resolve this, and how was the friendship affected by this problem?

a) How have friendships with shared power in decision-making felt differently from friendships that exhibited a parent-child power structure?

4. Can you think of a time when a friendship changed due to your girlfriend's competitiveness (or your own)? How did you go forward? Were you able to salvage the relationship or did it end?

5. As you look back on a friendship that has ended, are you able to also recall memories of fun times with this friend? Explain how you incorporate this friendship into your life story, and what part it plays in how you behave in current friendships.

6. How have previous friendships that have been difficult, painful, or disappointing colored your impression of female friendships and caused you to have trust issues in future friendships?

5

Connection, Communication, and Intimacy

Truly great friends are hard to find, difficult to leave, and impossible to forget.

G. Randolf

I have worked with hundreds of women who are hungry for a meaningful relationship with a female friend. They have shared their stories of disappointment or loneliness, and they are searching for the right tools to help them discover authentic, genuine, and healthy female relationships. In their quest for significant friendships with other women, my clients look for three things: *connection*, *communication*, and *intimacy*.

Connection

Happiness researchers have been trying for many decades to understand the recipe for what makes people happy. They have determined that happy people share a common thread: they are all well-connected to others; in other words, they are social.

Happiness has not been found to be correlated with income, but it *has* been highly correlated with social relationships (Diener & Seligman, 2004, 80–83). In a 2002 study of happiness in young people, Ed Diener, PhD, also known as "Dr. Happiness," and Martin Seligman, PhD, researchers in the field of positive psychology, screened 222 undergraduate students. Those with the highest scores of happiness and fewest signs of depression all had the same traits of strong connections to friends and family and commitment to sharing time with them (Diener & Seligman, 2002, 1–31).

Professor Nicholas Christakis, MD, director of the Human Nature Lab at Yale University, and James Fowler, PhD, associate professor at UC San Diego, are social scientists who conduct research on social factors affecting our health and longevity. Their findings, published in 2009 in *Connected: The Surprising Power of Our Social Networks and How They Shape Our Lives*, found that friends of happy people have a greater chance of being happy themselves. In other words, happiness is contagious, and friendship is one of the ways we spread this (Christakis & Fowler, 2009).

In her 2009 book *The Happiness Project*, *New York Times* bestselling author Gretchen Rubin lists many ways to boost our joy in life, but she is unwavering in her view that our friends play the most critical part in our quest for happiness. "One conclusion was blatantly clear from my happiness research," she writes, "everyone from contemporary scientists to ancient philosophers agrees that having strong social bonds is probably the *most* meaningful contributor to happiness" (Rubin, 2009, 141).

In other words, these researchers have all concluded from their findings that our friendships and our circle of connections do indeed matter greatly.

Created for Connection

The evidence is robust that we are happiest when we are connected to others. We seem to have an innate need to be in connection with others, and it is a common thread that is part of the human experience. And, when participating in these bonds that often span years, we benefit individually and collectively.

Is this human trait merely a coincidence? We each have to decide that for ourselves. In my opinion, it is important to also observe other species of nature in our attempt to understand the big picture. Whether or not you believe in a higher power, a deity, a creator, or a God of the universe, it is hard to argue with the many examples that demonstrate how we females have been designed to connect with our female friends.

Friendship Connections
Aren't Just for Humans

Humans are not the only species in which female friends are connected. In a recent study, published in the *Journal of Behavioral Ecology and Sociobiology* by Christian Ramp, PhD, and his team of scientists, female humpback whales of similar age reunited during six consecutive summers to feed and swim together in the Gulf of St. Lawrence off the Canadian coast. The female humpback friends that had the most stable and longest time as pairs also had the highest reproductive rates. (These bonds did not occur between similar-aged females and males, however.) Forming these long friendships clearly benefited the female humpbacks, as evidenced by their increased birth rates (Ramp et al, 2010, 1563–1576).

Connection means something different to women than it does to men. Men seem to be wired differently, and when they desire to connect, they participate in shared activities such as sports. Men enjoy spending time in side-by-side activities with each other as their method of communication in friendship. Women, on the other hand, have an inborn need to connect relationally and share emotionally. Women achieve intimacy and feel connected through sharing, self-disclosure, spending time together in face-to-face conversations, and showing kindness, empathy, and concern for each other.

Communication

Through today's social media world, there are numerous ways to communicate with our friends, unlike in the world I grew up in where the only phone was a landline and the only way to write to someone was through the U.S. Mail. In past decades, we had to pay expensive long-distance telephone rates to speak to our friends across the country. Staying in touch now is faster, easier, and more fun with Facebook, Instagram, Twitter, LinkedIn, Pinterest, email, Skype, FaceTime, and cell phones. This plethora of communication options makes staying in touch more feasible and, of course, much faster.

We have all heard the stories of how old friends from high school have reconnected on Facebook. More than ever before, today we can stay in close touch with our tribes, and social media have enriched many relationships that time and distance would have otherwise terminated. Technology has allowed the process of communicating regularly with friends to become instant, convenient, and affordable. This is a wonderful gift for keeping the fires of female friendships alive. Of course, being face-to-face with our girlfriends will always be our first choice, but when time, distance, and busy lives preclude that option, we are able to tap in to technology to achieve the next best thing.

Improving Communication with Friends

However, many of my clients still report they are not satisfied with the communication patterns or styles in their friendships. There are some key behaviors we can master to enhance the meaning and satisfaction in our female relationships. My top recommendations are listening, validating, and scheduling and sharing time.

Listening

A universal complaint I hear from women is that they don't feel their friends *listen* to them. This was listed frequently as a negative trait in the relationships of the women who responded to the questionnaires I distributed to gather data for this book. Some women mentioned wishing their friends would allow them to talk more and do a better job of listening to them. Many felt their friends often monopolized the conversations with their own problems. Another universal response from women was that they wished their girlfriends would "call me" and initiate the communication first some of the time. They reported that they are always the one who picks up the phone or reaches out, and they would like to see their friends do this first once in a while.

Becoming a good listener is a skill, and one that is worth honing. It involves maintaining good eye contact, not inter-rupting, and showing nonverbal cues which indicate that you care and are interested, such as leaning in and nodding your head. Resist the urge to bring the focus back to yourself by telling a story from your life experience, and just allow your friend to speak freely. Wanting to talk about oneself is a human tendency, but becoming a skilled listener will be worth every ounce of effort and endear you to your friends. I cannot emphasize this enough. If you are someone who deeply desires a circle of close girlfriends, begin with this critical step and become a five-star listener.

Validating

Another key communication tool is engaging in the act of *validating*. During difficult times, we receive great support and encouragement from people who enter into our painful world with us and offer words of validation. When your girlfriend is sharing her stories, her struggles, and explaining her storms in life, you can support her by offering validation. Making comments such as, "That must have been really hard for you," or "I can tell this situation is causing you a lot of emotional pain" sends a message of empathy and understanding. Validating someone's feelings is powerful, affirming, and, most important, *healing*.

Validation is an essential lifeline in our world of friendships, and one of the foundational building blocks for healthy, happy, and highly functioning relationships. You don't have to try to solve all of your girlfriend's problems; that is not what she needs right now. What you *can* do is listen, acknowledge that you see the issue as challenging, and assure her you will be there for her as she moves ahead. Validation sends the message of "I hear you, and I get it," and conveys the message that "You are not alone in this; I am here with you, too."

Scheduling and Sharing Time

When I distributed my questionnaire, one of the most common answers to the question, "Is there anything you would like to be different in any of your female friendships?" was the simple statement, "I wish we had more *time* together."

Many women explained that the challenges presented by distance were tough on special friendship connections, which was hard to accept and difficult to overcome. But as one respondent wrote, "Friendship means that no matter the time or the distance, we are always connected, and when we are together, it's like we've never been apart."

Respondents also mentioned that they wish they could make more time in their schedules to meet with girlfriends. We all know how difficult it is to carve out that time when we are juggling a dozen other balls. My suggestion is to find ways to intentionally schedule time with friends on a regular basis, much as we do for exercise, grocery shopping, or running errands. It is really about making this a new habit and part of your routine instead of allowing other activities and distractions to interfere with this essential time to share with your friends. There is no substitute for face-to-face time with our gal pals, and we need to reframe this by thinking of it as a necessity instead of a luxury.

The questionnaire answers reflect the ubiquitous attitude that women everywhere seem to share: we all crave more time with our female friends.

Intimacy

The last of the trio of traits women are longing for in their female friendships is the quality of intimacy, which is imperative to creating a relationship that is completely authentic and honest. Typically, the deeper we go into the inner circles of our friendships, the more emotionally intimate they naturally become. We have just discussed the essential elements of connection and communication, and intimacy completes the triangle of what women need and look for in their female friendships.

What does intimacy look like? How do we move toward having this in our relationships with our girlfriends?

Intimacy is an emotional attachment in a relationship shared by two people who enjoy closeness, familiarity, authenticity, and being together. With our women friends, we most typically experience the greatest intimacy in our inner circle and deeper, best-friend relationships, where we are confidants and share private and personal information. It does not usually exist in our more casual outer circle friendships or acquaintances (although there are always exceptions to this as people bond in mutual times of need or crisis).

Intimacy is born out of a mutual authenticity and vulnerability. As we build trust with each other, an openness to sharing as confidants follows. This results in the unearthing of our most raw parts, and we connect on a spiritual and emotional level. There is a core commitment to encourage and facilitate each other to be our best possible version. When we are authentic and genuine, the friendship continues to deepen and become more valuable. The unwavering trust that develops within this intimate bond becomes the glue that solidifies the relationship.

How do we move toward intimacy and actually experience it in our relationships with other women? Think about intimacy as the outcome of adding many levels of connection on top of a base foundation using the pyramid paradigm. As the friendship grows and moves toward a best friend-confidante, more levels are added moving upward toward intimacy. The foundation level is trust; everything else is built upon it. The levels above trust are honesty, authenticity, connectedness, vulnerability, reciprocal sharing, openness, and transparency. As these layers are added to the friendship one by one, the final level at the peak of the pyramid is reached, and this is intimacy.

Intimacy can operate on a continuum in our female friendships, as we may experience more modest degrees of intimacy with some of our inner circle of friends while achieving larger levels in a few of our best friendships.

Flaky Friends

Sometimes you'll encounter people who do not seem to value your friendship connection and do not embrace the healthy traits we have just covered in this chapter. You will be able to spot these "flaky friends" easily: they are the ones who repeatedly cancel lunch dates at the last minute, or talk about you behind your back, or cannot seem to ever be genuinely happy for you when good things come your way; the relationship with them is about as far from intimate as you can get. These people are probably not going to make good "besties," and you

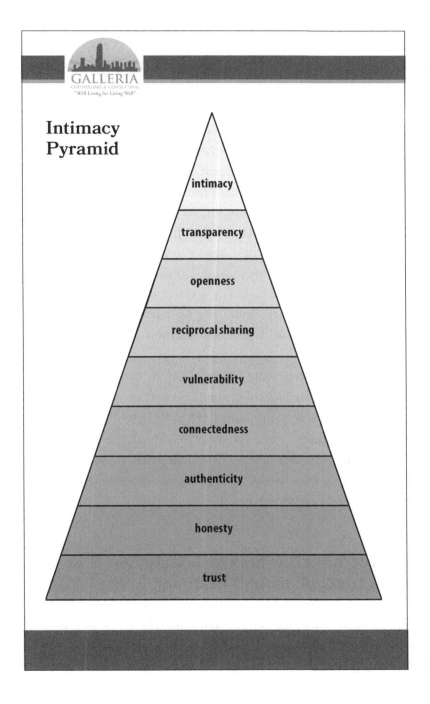

would be smart to keep them in the outer circles of friends or terminate the friendship altogether. They typically will be self-serving in the friendship, and they operate according to what best serves their own agenda.

Remember to pay attention to patterns; if you have been disappointed by all the last-minute canceled plans, understand that this will likely happen again. If your friend usually forgets to show up or cancels plans at the last minute, there may be something else going on. This may be anything from financial issues to poor time management and chronic disorganization to a substance abuse problem or anxiety at the prospect of going out in public. Depression, which causes people to withdraw and isolate from social situations, could be another possibility. Encouraging a friend to seek professional help is essential if a serious mental health problem is suspected.

No matter the issue, it does affect the friend who is impacted by these behaviors and is on the receiving end of the canceled lunch dates and other flaky behaviors. If the pattern continues, it is important to rethink the relationship and decide if you really want to be in it at all. If you do choose to stay in this friendship, then it is time for setting your own boundaries to protect yourself.

Overcoming Barriers to Connection, Communication, and Intimacy

When I give my weekend seminars on "The Healing Power of Girlfriends," we spend time sharing with each other in small groups. We discuss some of the challenges and barriers in building and keeping friendships. The participants find this exercise helpful because we scrutinize some of the typical pitfalls in maintaining female friendships.

There are definitely shared threads in the stories that are told. It is not surprising that one of the frequent barriers is finding enough *time* to connect and communicate in friendships. I know during the years I was raising my four kids and working on my degrees, if my schedule got crazy, the first thing I did was scratch out the lunch date with my girlfriend. In fact, time with friends should be the one event that we protect and guard with our very lives.

Another barrier that the women in my seminars find prevents connection and intimacy in female friendships is *life transitions*. We all know there is one thing in life we can count on, and that is change: nothing stays the same for long. Jobs change, people move around, kids grow up and leave home, we leave neighborhoods we have always lived in. These make up the life transitions we are all so familiar with, and they impact our routines, our families, and our friendships. When I think of the life transitions that define my adulthood, it makes my head spin.

Many women have revealed to me that as they go through different stages of life, the opportunities for making new friendships also changes. During some of our early years—in our early twenties, for instance—we may find ourselves in a rich environment such as a college campus, where meeting new people and making new friends is not a challenge. There are all kinds of groups to join such as sororities, or academic clubs or groups on campus that make it pretty much a given that you will make new connections, providing you the opportunity to form new friendships. After college, many young people find their new social groups through work connections or meetups in their free time.

There are exceptions to everything, but a lot of women report that these years are typically richer with opportunities for making new female friends.

Later years can be more challenging as different chapters of life bring new realities. A new job may require a move across the country to a state where you know no one. Or you may be in the chapter of new motherhood and feel isolated at home with little ones, with few windows of opportunity to make new friends. For empty nesters, a move to a new city may present a huge challenge to finding new friendships because the opportunities that arise from raising kids and connecting with other parents is now gone. And for older adults who find themselves in a new chapter of life, such as being a widow, the prospect of getting out and making new friends can be beyond overwhelming.

Tips for Overcoming Barriers

1. Assess the type of barrier impeding your ability to connect with your friends. If it is not having enough *time*, think about how to intentionally schedule regular "girlfriend time" into your calendar. *No excuses.* Look at it this way: your emotional and physical health will benefit from time spent with girlfriends, and remember that science is now telling us we live happier, healthier, and longer lives as a result.

2. If the barrier is *life transitions,* then what specific challenge is this presenting for you? Assess what in

particular is blocking your ability to connect with friends or make new friends. Once you've identified the obstacle, write down on paper some possible solutions, and then develop a plan for how to move toward those solutions. For instance, if you are a new widow and feel alone and disconnected, and you desire to make some new friends, brainstorm some ways to make that happen. Where are some places in your community you might find others similar to yourself who also wish to make new friends? Remember, you are not unique; there are others out there who also desire to connect and who are trying to find *you*. Yes, they are. So, whether you join a new book club, wine group, Bible study, travel club, knitting guild, or volunteer organization, start the process to find your tribe. Today is the day.

3. Make your girlfriend relationships a *priority*. One of the most common mistakes women make is to approach our female friendships with a casual, accidental, nonchalant, off-the-cuff, spur-of-the-moment attitude. Our friendships deserve better. We all deserve better.

    Many of my female clients have shared how they feel they have not made their female friendships priority. Women wear many hats and assume many roles that demand time, focus, and energy. Our girlfriends often fall at the bottom of the heap. Changing how we prioritize our time with our girlfriends begins in changing our thoughts and attitudes first. Don't give your girlfriends the leftover parts of yourself; make them a priority by intentionally scheduling time with them on a regular basis, and deliberately keep those connections alive. Your physical and emotional health will thank you.

Life transitions come and go as we move through new chapters of our lives. But for many people, these chapters bring challenges for making new friends along the way. The good news is, no matter how challenging our worlds become, or what stage of life we find ourselves in, there are still new friendship connections within our grasp. I'll discuss this more in the next chapter.

Impact of Transitions

My husband and I have moved for his career six times since we were married 40 years ago. We have built and sold multiple homes, lived in four states, had nine different addresses, and survived numerous career path changes for both us. Each time we invested our time and efforts into raising our four children, getting involved in their schools, activities, our communities, and church. Then, one day in the blink of an eye, our kids were grown and gone! We officially joined the new life transition category of "empty nesters."

Looking back over these many years of change, I quickly see how these transitions have impacted my friendships that now span numerous states and decades.

The relevant question becomes, "How do we maintain and hold on to friendships through all the transitions of life?" That is the challenge for all of us, but it is well worth the effort to figure out a solution and prioritize the friendships that are important. Geography does dictate how easily it is to stay in touch with our friends when we move away; however, it does not have to end the relationship if both people are committed to staying in touch. This goes back to the concepts of *communication, connection,* and *intimacy* in friendship. When there is a shared desire by both friends to continue the relationship, even while being separated by several states, it is possible to continue to enjoy the friendship. It has to be mutual and a priority for both parties or it does not work.

What I have witnessed is that for some of my friendships, my move to a new state actually served to make us value the friendship more and put forth a bigger effort to stay in touch over the miles. We no longer took our time together for granted, nor did we choose to let the miles dictate our emotional closeness. Although we were no longer able to meet for lunch and share our friend time face-to-face, we made it a priority to call, email, and send cards and notes on a regular basis. Spontaneity was replaced by a deliberate effort to keep the friendship alive and well.

It is my hope that this chapter has highlighted the merits of connection, communication, and intimacy in female friendships. We women have been wired to connect with each other, and when we embrace that completely in our female friendships, we benefit in a myriad of ways. Through our strong efforts to strive for healthy communication by listening, validating, and sharing time, we can enjoy closer connections and achieve a much richer and greater depth of emotional intimacy with our girlfriends.

DISCUSSION QUESTIONS

1. One of the barriers we experience in connecting with our friends is a lack of time. Discuss an example of when you were in a time crunch and you took a social meetup with your girlfriend off your calendar, or maybe told her you did not have time to connect.

   a) Knowing how essential to our health our connections with our girlfriends are, how might you make a different choice or prioritize your time differently now?

2. Another barrier to connection, communication, and intimacy that was discussed in this chapter is life transitions. Think of a time when a move or other life transition created a challenge in your friendships.

   a) How did you overcome these barriers, or did you?

   b) Was your friendship affected by these challenges? If so, how did you deal with this?

   c) How does geography affect your friendships now?

3. How has social media and technology (Facetime, Skype, text messaging) changed your connections with girl-friends today?

   a) Overall, would you say that social media has a positive effect on your friendships and how you stay in connection and communication with them? Explain.

4. When was a time you were disappointed in a friendship that turned out to be with a "flaky friend" instead of a dependable, stable, and loyal friend? (I've defined "flaky" as someone who cancels your meetups at the last minute regularly, gossips about you behind your back, is envious of you when good things happen to you, etc.)

   a) Explain how you dealt with this, and were you able to stay in the relationship?

   b) How did this change your perspectives for future friendships?

How Do We Make New Friends?

Friendship improves happiness, and abates misery, by doubling our joy and dividing our grief.

Marcus Tullius Cicero

One of the common questions I get from women is "How do I make new friends?" The desire to make new friends—while feeling it is next to impossible—is almost ubiquitous. The passion to write this book was born from a deep desire to help women forge ahead to seek and form new friendship connections. For many people that process can be challenging for a multitude of reasons...but in the end, the result is the same. We feel alone, disconnected, and isolated without a circle of friends to support us, encourage us, and to share life with us. That doesn't need to be the case. There are numerous ways to create a supportive circle of friends. But first you might need to step outside of your comfort zone.

Get Out of Your Comfort Zone

Several years ago, a new client named Donna, who was a middle-aged empty nester, walked into my counseling office and shared with me, "I am here to learn how to make new friends. I feel lonely and do not have close girlfriends. Please help me—I am desperate to be like other ladies and have girlfriends to hang out, go to lunch, and just share life with."

Donna and I talked about her interests and hobbies and discussed what ways she might meet people and find some new, meaningful female friendships. I helped her formulate a plan to get out of her comfort zone and risk a bit; after all, what did she have to lose?

Donna had been waiting for women to *find her*. She was more of an introvert and rather reserved. She had not really been successful at taking any action steps to meet new women, so we brainstormed some ways she could put herself "out there" and meet some fun, new people. I suggested she embrace this statement as her new motto: "This first attempt may or may not work, and we may or may not become friends, and it is really okay—at least I tried."

She slowly did begin to become more comfortable with meeting people and taking a risk. I encouraged her—as I encourage you—to stay positive and hopeful, even if the first attempt does not work out or the second meetup is a "no go"—just stay in the game and do not get discouraged, as eventually you will meet someone who, just like you, is looking for a special friend to share life with.

I know from my own experiences that it works to push ourselves to get out there and try new friend groups and new meetups. I believe in these tactics and have seen how they have worked in my own life. I don't ask people to do things I don't believe in, so I can honestly say that these approaches do deliver new friends. If you'd like additional suggestions, visit my website at http://GalleriaCounseling.com.

Let me give you a recent, personal example that has been a true blessing and a gold mine for finding a wonderful new group of girlfriends. About a year ago, I saw an invitation on our neighborhood Nextdoor app on my phone. (Nextdoor is a private social network for neighborhood communities.) A woman in the neighborhood asked if other women would like to help her start a new wine meetup group in our area, centered around fellowship, fun, food, and, of course, wine. I signed up for this right away because I was rather new in the area, and I had not yet met lots of new neighbors other than a few wonderful women on my street. Well, here we are, about eighteen months later, and I have a group of the most kind, fun, and fabulous new friends. It was worth every ounce of the effort and anxiety to push myself to get out there and just go for it. I never thought I would be making such dear friendships in these empty-nester years. So never give up, and keep in mind another one of my favorite mantras: "Not all wonderful things in our lives happen in our youth." There are new girlfriends out there waiting to meet you.

Practical Tools for Getting Out of Your Comfort Zone

What are the best tools for making new girlfriends? Here are my top six suggestions to help you jump-start your new friendship connections:

- Be a Joiner
- Find Support Groups
- Follow the Friendship Path
- Pursue a Volunteer Cause
- Say YES to Invitations
- Make Connections with Coworkers

In both my own personal experience and in working with clients, I've found pursuing one or more of these options leads to meeting new women and creating opportunities for deep and lasting friendships.

Be a Joiner. One of the main ways that people have the opportunity to meet new people is to find a group based on a shared interest. These might include book, wine, or cooking clubs, Zumba, yoga, or other exercise classes, knitting guilds, church or Bible study groups, mom groups, walking or biking groups, golf, tennis, or other sports groups, or singles meetups. Out of a shared interest comes an incredible opportunity to make new friends who like the same activities. Within these new groups, new connections and intimacies are formed, and new friendships are born that often result in treasured, forever bonds. But it takes one very important first step: you must reach out and search for a new group, dive in, and go for it!

Lifetime Benefits of Joining a New Group

When we moved to Texas many years ago, I had the honor and pleasure of making many special friendships after joining our neighborhood church. Through the years, these special friendships have grown and blossomed into lasting and loyal relationships. We have watched our kids grow up together in our community, go off to college, get married, and begin careers and families. These girlfriends are special for so many reasons, not the least of which is that we share such a rich history of raising our kids in the same community. Whether it was hosting bridal or baby showers for each other's young adult children, or meeting up for our birthday lunches, we have all enjoyed walking the path of female friendship together. These wonderful friends were the outcome of taking the first step to join a new church group.

Many women have shared with me that finding a group to join actually was the kindest gift they ever gave themselves. As they have looked back on the rich friendships that came out of these new groups, they have concluded that the risk of putting themselves out there beyond their comfort zones was worth every ounce of fear or doubt they had to confront and silence. One of the young moms who filled out my female friendship questionnaire shared that she is one of eight friends who are all moms and provide each other with support and encouragement. She did not have this group when she had her first two babies, and she added that being a mom is so much easier and better now with the help of amazing friends.

MOPS International: Support for Young Moms

One example of a women's group is MOPS (Mothers of Preschoolers) International, a young mothers' group that offers support, fellowship, and friendship. I have had the privilege of being a guest speaker at numerous MOPS groups over the years.

These young women seem to share a rather universal experience: they joined this group to make friends and feel less isolated. Many of them have spoken of just moving to a new state and feeling alone and lonely, until they made new connections through MOPS. I have heard comments such as, "I left such a wonderful circle of girlfriends in my old state, and I was feeling a deep void until I made some new friends in this new mom's group. They have made all the difference and have truly been a gift."

Find Support Groups. I have run support groups for women in my clinical practice for many years. I have witnessed how women can come together, and how, through trust and friendship, total strangers can become confidants. The connections made and the bonds formed become the fertile ground where emotional growth and healing take root. Being a therapist has given me a front row seat to watch how women can heal their wounds, discover a strength they did not know they possessed, and become the best versions of themselves through the special connections and friendships they discover in support groups. It is life transforming to share with those we trust, and this only underscores the need we all have for fellowship and human connection. Here are some ideas for finding a support group near you:

1. Check websites of counseling offices in your area; many of them offer support groups for women.
2. If you are a young mother (stay-at-home or working outside the home) search the internet for meetup groups in your area. MOPS groups are located in all 50 states and in many international countries.
3. Many hospitals offer different types of support groups for women as part of their health education and wellness programs.
4. If you are a new mom and would benefit from a postpartum or breastfeeding support group, those are also wonderful ways to connect with others who are at a similar place in their lives. Many women's hospitals or OB units also have a list for these groups.

5. Churches often offer support groups specifically for women, and especially for people going through difficult times due to grief or loss.

6. Support groups exist for a variety of activities and interests, from exercise training to writers who aspire to become published authors. Finding support is a matter of finding your tribe, and seeking those who are looking for the same type of support.

Follow the Friendship Path. Another proven tactic for finding new friends is to follow the friendship path from our own friends to their other friends. Most of the time our friends will have common traits, values, and personalities similar to, or that mesh with, those of their other trusted friends, so it makes sense we would find a natural connection with these new people. I have heard many women share their stories of how they were introduced to their best friend's girlfriends, hit it off immediately, and now have become close friends with them, too.

Never underestimate the opportunity to make new friends that may be right in front of you. If you find yourself lucky enough to be invited to a party, an event, or any lunch meetup with your bestie, seize the chance to be introduced to some wonderful new potential friends. There are no accidents in life, and when God opens the door of friendship for you, don't pass up this golden opportunity to walk through it.

Pursue a Volunteer Cause. Many people have made new and endearing friendships through finding a place to volunteer. Giving time to a cause or charity, and spending time with other volunteers who share this passion to make a difference and donate their time, is a great way to meet like-minded people and form new connections. Serving others is an opportunity to meet new friends who also share this value as an important gift to humanity. Whether it is volunteering at a hospital, a food bank, a homeless shelter, the airport, a nursing home, or a mental health organization, the potential to make connections and establish new friendships is a common link.

Say YES to Invitations. If you are fortunate to be on the receiving end of social invitations, try to say yes whenever possible. Many people don't realize that if they repeatedly say no to invitations, those invitations may stop coming their direction. And by attending a party, event, lunch, dinner, or after-work meetup, you are putting yourself in the "I may make a new friend today" chair at the table. Each invitation can be viewed as a golden opportunity to make an amazing new connection and possibly a future treasured friend. All it requires is for you to put yourself out there, take a chance, and go for it.

Coworker Connections. One of the richest environments for making new female friendships is at work. It is not surprising that common bonds develop in the workplace, as people spend many hours together and share their life stories at lunch or over a cup of coffee during the day. The connections made often last long after jobs have changed and people have moved on.

I can honestly say that coworker connections that lead to lasting lifetime friendships are not a myth. They indeed happen, and the girlfriends I now have today from my professional life through the years are gifts beyond measure. My clients have also told stories of deep friendships they have made while at work, and several of these friendships have continued on through many chapters of their lives and into retirement years. It seems that sharing a profession at work provides a perfect framework for a girlfriend connection to emerge and to thrive for many years to come. One responder to my questionnaire wrote that in the beginning, coworker friendships are born out of a cohesive working relationship, but they blossom into much more as the connection moves out of the workplace and into the social world.

Too Old to Make New Friends?

For those of you who insist you may be too old to make new friends, I share my sincere belief that we are never too old to participate in the gift of a new friendship with another. I have witnessed this with older clients as well as with my own mother-in-law, all of whom moved to retirement communities in their seventies and eighties.

One of the key components we have found to be linked with longevity is resilience—the ability to adapt as life changes around us. Watching these elderly ladies quickly adapt to their new surroundings and thrive in them gave me pause. The point of connection between all of these ladies was that they all made new female friends in their new retirement homes rather quickly. They took advantage of social gatherings such as game and movie nights, happy hour, and group trips to shopping and local arts performances. As we discussed in Chapter 2, having friends as we grow older is key to our health and happiness.

Let me share my own story of a wonderful new friend who moved in next door to us after we moved to a new community several years ago. Although Megan is young enough to be my daughter, she has quickly become a dear and special friend to me. She is a source of sweet camaraderie, support, kindness, and caring.

When our daughter's home was badly flooded in Hurricane Harvey, Megan joined us (as did our other wonderful neighbors) to help wash the kitchen items that were salvaged. This act of love and friendship will forever be etched in my soul. A true friend springs into action during times of tragedy and need, and shares the struggles and burdens with you.

This story highlights two main points I have been making in this book. First, the opportunities to make new friends are all around us, so be open to them and seize them when they are presented. Second, the gift of friendship transcends generations and age groups. Don't close the door on the potential for a new friendship with a much younger or older person because you may be losing out on a truly amazing connection that will bring you great joy and happiness.

Being able to reach out and make new friends is valuable, whether you are 29 or 89. We are never too old to discover the gift of a new friendship.

DISCUSSION QUESTIONS

1. Can you think of a time in your life when making new friends was especially difficult? How did you overcome the challenge of making new friends during this time, or did you?

2. Have transitions in your life made making new friends more challenging? Explain.

3. When was a time you became a "joiner" and reached out to a new group to make new girlfriends?

   a) What came out of that experience for you in terms of personal growth?

   b) If someone was thinking of getting out of their comfort zone and wanted to join a new group, what would you tell them about this experience based on what you have learned from your own?

4. Have you ever followed the "friendship path" to making new girlfriends by meeting friends of friends?

   a) Did some good friendships come out of this? Explain.

b) How would you encourage another woman to try this option to making new friends?

5. Discuss a time when you were invited to a social gathering that you really did not care to go to. Did you go ahead and push yourself to go anyway? If so, did you meet any potential new girlfriends at this event?

6. Have you made new friendships through work connections or professional groups? If so, explain how the friendship started and how it has evolved from a work relationship to a girlfriend status.

a) As career paths change and jobs also take new turns, has the friendship continued and survived these new chapters of life? Explain.

b) As you have aged, has making friends become easier or more difficult?

c) If you are a senior adult (or know someone who is), how have friendships had a positive effect on well-being and happiness for you (or for that person) in this chapter of life?

7

What Do You Bring to the Friendship Table?

A friend loves at all times.

Proverbs 17:17

One of the questions I asked women on my friendship questionnaire was, "What do you think you bring to your friendships with other women?" It is a very relevant question because all women have the opportunity to play a part in someone's friendship story. Thinking about what we contribute helps us to focus on our responsibility as a girlfriend to make a difference in someone's life. So although many women told me they had never given much thought to this self-examination question, the purpose of asking it was to prompt the respondents to pause and assess the ways they participate in their friendships. The answers were insightful and revealing; women shared from their hearts what they bring to their friendships. Though varied, the responses show how deep and meaningful friendships can be. Here are a few:

- I'm open-minded and a good listener. I'm honest. I always have wine.
- I bring transparency, honesty, and support.
- When asked to keep something in confidence, I'm 100 percent trustworthy.
- Hugs! Never underestimate a hug to show you care. I try to listen actively.

Common themes connect these responses. Healthy, meaningful friendships don't just happen; they are the product of deliberate and intentional efforts to nurture the relationship and prioritize the well-being of the other person.

Many of these women consider the quality of "giving of myself when someone is in need" to be the most valuable aspect they bring to a friendship. Whether your friend needs support physically or emotionally, you are in a unique position to be her beacon of hope. Here's how some of the respondents described this quality:

- I am available in whatever way the other person needs—a listening ear, advice, a lunch buddy, shopping partner, or spiritual advisor.
- I am very optimistic and upbeat by nature, so I hope to be able to lift friends, especially in their time of need.
- I am inquisitive, curious, compassionate, understanding, forgiving, and able to overlook quirks. I am not easily offended.

If you have not previously considered the question of what you bring to the friendship table, I challenge you to do so now. Sit down and spend some time in quiet reflection to examine your friendships and what traits and qualities you bring to those relationships.

When True Healing Is Needed

We all know that part of life is getting hit with curveballs. They come when we least expect them, and they take the wind out of our sails. I speak from experience; my life has been defined by them.

For instance, I was only 35 when my husband's health challenges almost made me a widow with four kids to raise alone. This experience left me feeling pretty vulnerable and shaky. I remember how wounded I felt . . . and I especially remember the healing that followed from the care and support I received from my girlfriends. They brought in meals for our family; they took our kids while I went with my husband to his doctor appointments. Sometimes they just stopped in to check on us and see what we needed. They took me to lunch when things calmed down and gave me a chance to just breathe. These were acts of love, empathy, care and concern, and kindness, and most importantly, they were *healing*. They helped me get through a very difficult time in my life when I was running out of fuel. I knew I was not alone, and these female friends would walk through this valley with me until we were safely on the other side. They were my angels of healing.

What I see clearly from the questionnaire responses to this question is that true healing comes from sitting at the table of friendship with our girlfriends—sometimes literally. Here is where we can come "just as we are" and receive support, unconditional love, forgiveness, compassion, understanding, encouragement, loyalty, empathy, advice—if we want it—and honesty that is free of judgment. Here is where we can be raw, totally genuine, and authentic, and receive the healing that comes from connecting with our girlfriends. Here is where we can find a safe place to just breathe and let our guard down, and to share our burdens, deepest secrets, biggest fears, and darkest moments.

The Three "Rs" of Healing

Life can be challenging, even traumatic, as events unfold that we can neither stop nor alter. Part of the human experience is that sooner or later we will find ourselves or those we love on the receiving end of loss, hardship, or tragedy. Some of our biggest assets during these times will be our girlfriends. It is within those female friendships where we will find three parts of the healing process.

Through the three Rs—Repair, Restoration, and Recovery—you can help your girlfriend find the path back from her wounded, hurting, and scarred self.

Repair

The first step toward healing begins with the process of assessing the damage so we can focus our efforts on where they will do the most good. Offer reassurance and encouragement to your friend to communicate that you will walk this path with her, and let her know she is not alone. Being a good listener who offers support is a highly valued trait for women in friendships, and there is no better time to show those strengths than to focus on helping a friend repair whatever hurt she has suffered. Here are some ways to do that:

- Verbalize to your friend that she is not alone and that you are here to offer a nonjudgmental listening ear.
- Reassure her that you will share this time of healing and act as her "wingman" in the days ahead.
- Provide her with the opportunity to feel safe so that she may vent, grieve, cry, express anger or frustration, and share her true emotions.

Restoration

The next step is about helping with rebuilding and moving toward strength and empowerment again. Those are often the first qualities to go, and losing them can create a sense of helplessness, hopelessness, anxiety, and vulnerability. If your friend is feeling fragile, exhausted, or tapped out (as we often do following a traumatic or difficult event), offer your time and resources to assist her with getting her life back on track. We feel best when we are in the comfort zone of our regular schedules, so this is often as simple as helping her find her "new normal." Here are some ways to provide support:

- Ask your girlfriend how you can best assist in the daily routines, whether it is to bring meals, provide childcare, run errands, do laundry, or go to the grocery store.

- Offer to pick her up and treat her to lunch or dinner to provide some much-needed rest and relaxation.
- Ask if you can provide a "taxi" service if she needs to go to doctor appointments or her children need rides to activities.
- Enlist the help of her other family or friends (with her approval) who may also want to offer assistance during this restoration process.

Recovery

The last step in the healing process is about your girlfriend actually returning to her normal state of functioning. In this stage, autonomy and independence begin to show up again. Old routines return, or she embraces the new ones she's created through the restoration process.

Girlfriends are key in this last phase of healing because they can keep a watchful eye on their friend's progress and continue to support her when needed. As emotional, mental, and physical healing occurs, female friends continue to play a vital role, one of encouragement and connection.

Here are some ways to help:

- Check in with her daily or several times a week to see what her needs are and if anyone can be of assistance.
- Offer her time to talk, vent, or share via phone or face-to-face so that she maintains critical connections.
- Watch for signs of unexpected or delayed stress and fatigue that may not have presented before (for

example, if she is having sleeping issues or you notice mood swings).

- Continue to encourage, support, and mentor her in the recovery process by being positive, helpful, and exhibiting acts of kindness and compassion.

These three Rs equip us with tools to help our female friends heal, and we have been perfectly designed by God to share them. The gifts you bring to the friendship table may just be the exact gifts your girlfriend needs to begin.

Helping A Girlfriend Find Her Way Back from Challenges

Every friendship is unique, so trust your instincts about what your girlfriend values and needs from you in these moments of healing. In addition, let me offer some *specific* healing components that I recommend to begin the process of the repair work:

1. Allow your girlfriend the time to tell her story and share the issues that are causing her pain. Be fully present with her during this time, and listen with empathy and compassion. This is key: resist the urge to turn the conversation back to yourself and your story, and let her share openly. As one woman wrote, "[I offer] candor and an open mind, as well as being a good listener. The good listener, I think, is a challenge for most of us, to fight the urge to implement our own opinions."

2. Validate her feelings and emotions. Communicate to her that she is not alone and you are there to share her burdens, hurts, and fears. Meet her where she is in her struggles emotionally and spiritually. One questionnaire respondent wrote, "I listen, and I help by supporting friends in whatever they may be going through at the time." Another called herself a "good listener . . . even to the wee hours of the morning. Encourager, loyal, good discernment, thoughtful, kind, supportive, trustworthy, generous heart, willing to share my faith walk with my Lord and Savior. I can turn into a tiger if my girlfriend is in trouble!" Listening plus validating is a very powerful combination.

3. Ask her how you can be the most helpful during this time and what would support her the most; for example, does she want you to pray with her, or help with hands-on tasks such as child care, preparing meals, or checking in with her daily?

4. When she is ready, help her to reframe the situation so she can see hope and healing in the near future. Find some positives that she can grab on to, and help her see some possible solutions that are within reach. In other words, help her find "the silver lining." (Sometimes we have to look hard to find it, I know.) I have a girlfriend who has experienced more than her fair share of loss. She knows the pain of losing loved ones as a young adult and then suffering more loss later in life through divorce. However, she has raised truly amazing children. We spoke not long ago about all of this, and when she became extremely negative about her life, I reframed things for her quickly. I reminded

her of the silver lining—that she had produced three accomplished, smart, and successful young adults, who clearly will continue to be very bright stars in her sky. She readily agreed and quickly replied that I was right, and she just needed that friendly reminder of how blessed she really is despite the many setbacks she has endured.

5. Check in with her regularly and frequently so she knows you are not abandoning her. As a respondent wrote, "I offer unconditional loyalty. If I call you my friend, I will be there whenever and wherever you need me to be." You are there for the long haul, and you want her to know she can count on that.

6. Plan a girlfriend celebration together to acknowledge her progress on the road to recovery and repair. When she feels ready, celebrate her hard work to heal from her difficult time. Help her see how far she has come from the struggles and the darkness to step into the light of healing and renewal. Even if she has only been able to take baby steps, it is essential to acknowledge progress with her.

Be Someone's Angel

Don't ever underestimate the power you have as someone's girlfriend to be their angel, their lifeline, and their anchor.

Let me share a real-life example of this from my own friendship history. While having lunch a few years ago and literally sitting at the friendship table with Alicia, a beloved girlfriend, she handed me a wrapped gift as we sipped our coffee. When I opened this thoughtful gift, I saw a lovely gold chain necklace with a little anchor medallion. It was packaged with this verse:

FRIENDSHIP

Make a wish and put on your necklace;
True friends give us something to hold
onto and help us stay afloat.
Wear your necklace as a reminder
that you are my anchor.[1]

As I started to tear up, my girlfriend smiled and said, "This is a perfect gift for you, since you are my anchor." I was so honored, and so blown away! It had never occurred to me that she saw me in that way. We always have been very open, sharing easily with each other, and even though I was more than a decade her senior, we could relate on many fronts with our lives as moms, wives, and women.

So I learned a life lesson that day. Never assume you aren't playing a vital part in someone's life just because you may not be aware of it. Never take for granted the opportunity you have as a girlfriend to be someone's anchor in their storm. Never underestimate that God will use you to be someone's angel at just the right moment, in just the right way.

You just may find yourself—as I did that day at lunch with my girlfriend—in shock and saying with awe, "Who . . . me?"

---

1 Anchor necklace is handcrafted in the U.S.A. by the DOGEARED® Company.

DISCUSSION QUESTIONS

1. What do you think you bring to the table of friendship with other women?

    a) How might your girlfriends answer this question about you?

    b) How has reading this book and learning more about what women want from their girlfriends changed how you might be in the future?

2. Have you ever walked through a difficult time with your girlfriend's struggles? How do you think you made a difference for her during this time?

3. What, if anything, would you like to be different in your female friendships?

4. Have you ever felt that geography has gotten in the way of your female friendships? Explain how you have dealt with this situation.

    a) Is there a way you might improve how you deal with geography challenges in the future?

5. How do you deal with the challenge of not having enough time to connect with your girlfriends?

   a) Are you the one who usually reaches out to connect first? Explain.

   b) How can you do a better job of connecting with so little time in your busy life?

6. Have you ever had the unexpected honor to learn you were a girlfriend's angel, anchor, or lifeline in a storm? Explain how that made you feel and how it has affected you going forward in your friendships.

8

Female Friendship Is God's Perfect Gift

Friendship is the inexpressible comfort of feeling safe with a person,
having neither to weigh thoughts nor measure words.

Dinah Craik

The opportunity to keep adding to your tapestry of life with meaningful relationships and rich experiences is one of the beauties of growing older. You also acquire wisdom and a large frame of reference that serve to create a sophisticated sense of savvy. In our American culture that seems to idolize youth, what we find out later is that much of our beauty is actually acquired from living through the seasons of life.

Over the years we learn, stumble, fall down, get up, grow, renew, heal, forgive, start over, repair, become resilient, and finally soar. These trials and tribulations give us a valuable frame of reference that provides a beacon of light for our future path. Our friendships are an integral part of this journey, and they serve as a compass to guide us and keep us balanced, focused, and safely in the channel where we will not drift off course. As we are tossed about and endure the waves of life, we often become aware that we are surrounded by others who are keeping us afloat in the storm. These are our circle of friends who have a core commitment to our safety and well-being. They breathe life into our souls when we are too tired to take another breath. They fuel our engines when we are running on empty, and they keep us upright when the wind has been taken out of our sails and we are in danger of running aground.

Equally as valuable in our relationships is spreading joy and celebrating the good times. Yes, we need support during the darkness, but delighting in our happy days and magical moments together is priceless.

One of my greatest joys recently has been reveling in a new role with my other girlfriends who also are in, or about to be in, the "grandma club." When recognizing milestones, whether it is our kids' graduations, weddings, new grandbabies, significant birthdays (the ones that end in "0"), or just day-to-day lunch meetups and girls' nights out, the good times enrich our lives in a myriad of ways.

In this final chapter, the other point I would like to make is that there are no accidents in life. As I am beginning my seventh decade while putting this book together, I can tell you that I have lived long enough to see and live through a lot. You may call it a perfect alignment of the stars, some special force of energy, or, as I like to view it, God ordaining events to happen just as they are meant to—at the perfect time and in the perfect way. Throughout my life journey, I have continually been amazed by how just the right friend will remain by my side to hold me up at precisely the right moment in time. Coincidence? I think not. In fact, to see coincidence as the most likely conclusion would be short-sighted and rather simplistic, in my opinion. I choose to go for a much deeper meaning, a more intricate and complex line of logic.

There are many examples in my lifetime of events lining up just right. I cannot deny them nor pretend they do not exist. There is something much more massive out there, which defies comprehension. It is ever-present and all-knowing, a force beyond all human limitations, which is right there, at the exact moment we need it to be. It never disappoints; it never fails. It runs through all I am and all I know. For me, there is no dispute; I have seen too much. For me, it is my God.

When I say it never disappoints, I am not implying for a New York minute that things always turn out the way I want, nor do they always turn out to be easier, or more positive or perfect. To the contrary—sometimes events turn out completely opposite of how I wanted them to, or the path that opens up in front of me is much more challenging and difficult than I expected. But what I am offering here is that something really good and really powerful can come out of these situations, because there is a divine plan. I find comfort in this, and it gives me a sense of confidence and hope in knowing that no matter what, all will be okay. Looking at the big picture is reassuring because we can see quickly that we are but a tiny speck on the map, and a much larger force is at play. In reality, it is a myth to think we possess the keys of control over every facet of our destiny.

The Added Value of Female Friendships

I remember writing papers in my college philosophy classes and exploring questions such as "Why are we here?" and "What is our real purpose in life anyway?" I suppose there are as many different answers to this as there are people on the planet. Whatever you believe and however you may answer this question, I do embrace the fact that we were not put here to live in isolation. As I've mentioned previously, I believe that our creator designed us uniquely to be in communication with others. As one questionnaire respondent wrote, "[Friends are] people that God sends us to love, share, and support along our journey."

Research continues to highlight this finding and prove how much happier, healthier, and longer we live when we have communion with others. We function best when we are linked to others because that is how biology has stacked the deck. God has created us to live a life in relationship with others, and when we embrace that connection, we can benefit physically, emotionally, and spiritually. Another questionnaire respondent put this eloquently:

Friendship. My first thoughts drift toward creation as I consider the first relationship between God and man. I think of the makeup of our design, that we were not meant to be alone but in relationship with others. But not just meaningless encounters with strangers; we were designed to care, invest, and share love with one another. Friendships are those relationships that help us do those things (grow, love, care, and invest). They give value to life and remind me of the importance of our design to be in relationship with others and our creator.

One of the assets of those vital connections is that they elevate us to a new level of enjoying life and help embellish our existence in ways we could not have ever imagined. In particular, our girlfriend connections fill in the gaps of life, give us validation, and help us create the best version of ourselves. And most importantly, our girlfriend connections bring with them the powerful art of healing.

You can feel the healing and the change it creates in your head and your heart. When you walk through your pain holding the hand of a girlfriend, you are no longer alone, no longer lost, and no longer in a downward spiral. Perhaps this is because your friend will carry you when there is no strength left to walk. Her presence and outstretched arms serve to stabilize you and keep you going. You find healing in this moment, in this connection, in this special friendship, as she enters your pain with you. And, on the other side of it all, when the seas have calmed, the winds have ceased, and storms have passed, you realize you have found a new place of healing in your soul—a place centered on growth, on stretching you in new ways, as you push toward safety and security.

Many times you will not even realize what has taken place until after the fact. When you are in the middle of the chaos, you cannot always see the long view. Often it is in looking in the rearview mirror that you put all the pieces together and see how your survival was set into motion by the connection with your girlfriend. You see the powerful healing that results from sharing that friendship connection in that moment.

I would like to leave you with these final thoughts.

Prioritize your relationships with girlfriends as an important part of your human existence. *No excuses!* You are worth it! Nurture them, give them focus, time, effort, and value them as you would a priceless treasure. For it is in these powerful friendships that you will find a more meaningful existence, an invaluable life connection, and a happier and healthier version of yourself. It is in these friendships with your girlfriends that you will find true healing when it is needed. And, yes, there will be times you will need healing.

In working with a variety of women in my counseling practice for nearly 20 years, I can honestly conclude the following: Though we may be from different social, economic, ethnic, educational, and religious backgrounds, we *all* share a common thread as women. This common thread knows no color, no ethnicity, no economic or religious status. As women, we *all* are wired exactly the same to need fellowship with each other. Some of us may need lots of friends and others may prefer only a few close girlfriends. But what seems to link us all is the biological need to gather and connect with each other. The imprint that is left on our hearts and souls from these female friendships is penetrating, life-changing, and lasting. We women find the best version of ourselves when we share in female friendships.

DISCUSSION QUESTIONS

1. Can you think of a time when God placed just the right friend on your path at just the right moment in time? Explain.

2. When was a time that you needed healing in your life—emotionally, physically, or spiritually? Explain how your girlfriend carried you through this or held your hand as you walked through this difficult period.

3. Since God has created us to be in connection with our girlfriends, how can you make a bigger effort to give this a higher priority in your life?

4. Name some ways you see that women are similar in how they are wired to need fellowship with each other.

9

ℓasting ℓegacies in ℱriendship

Everyone wants to ride with you in the limo, but what you want is someone who will take the bus with you when the limo breaks down.

Oprah Winfrey

One of the blessings of being at the stage of life I am now, as an empty nester, is the luxury of having more free time to focus on my friends and connecting with them. We are now able to enjoy our friendships by staying in regular communication, often even planning trips together. It is such a gift to share a common history that spans many decades. A couple of these dear friends have passed away now, and their passing has left a hole in my heart forever. But the memories of those precious times together are woven in the tapestry of my life. These special ladies have left their mark on me in a myriad of ways, and I will always be grateful for how these friendships have shaped me into the woman and friend that I am today.

This book on friendship would not be complete if I did not share a few of my personal stories about the power of our girlfriends to help shape the people we become. I would be remiss if I did not digress briefly to include their prevailing influences on my life journey.

Nurse Friends

Kim

Reflecting on my single days and the girlfriends who were in my life, I cherish my fond memories of all the fun that comes with that glorious chapter. As a young and single RN in Omaha, many of my close friends were also nurses. We worked hard and played hard in those days. In fact, it was Kim, one of those dear nurse friends, who played Cupid and helped facilitate my first date with my now-husband. Kim knew him and hung out with many of his friends. After he and I were introduced at work, he asked her for my phone number, and the rest is history. I am grateful to Kim for her part in our romantic story, and she remains in my inner circle of close friends to this day.

Julie

A very close friend of mine who passed away far too young was Julie. We were both RNs working the night shift on the OB/GYN floor in the hospital in Omaha. She was always a breath of fresh air and started our shift every night with a huge smile on her face. I have fond memories of her mentoring me and helping me learn the ropes in the special care nursery (SCN) at night. She was kind, patient, compassionate, and an excellent nurse. Julie delivered meticulous care to every single tiny patient in the SCN. She was incredibly organized and gifted, and I used to marvel at the way she handled the tiny preemies with such ease and tender care. She was intelligent and dedicated, a role model for all nurses to emulate.

We became close friends as we worked those night shifts together, and she taught me so much about nursing, about life, and about mothering. Julie had two small children during those years, and I was amazed as I watched her balance being a full-time, dedicated mom and a busy OB nurse.

Julie was a trusted confidant and loyal girlfriend who I miss every single day. But what lingers now are the life lessons she left with us as her legacy. She always gave everything her strongest effort and strove for excellence. Whether it was her work with the preemies in the SCN or helping her own children learn a new skill, she had no use for laziness or complacency. Her zest for living life was contagious, and caring for all of God's creations, big or small, young or old, rich or poor, was her mission. It was obvious to all of us that nursing was a calling for her, not just a job, not just a paycheck, not just a profession. It was her destiny. She modeled for all of us how to deliver compassionate care that was generated from a special place deep in her heart.

During the time we worked together, I became engaged and started to plan my wedding. I asked Julie to be a bridesmaid and her darling daughter to be a flower girl. Although later the miles would separate us as I moved to other states with my husband, Julie and I continued to stay connected through cards, letters, and calls. Through the decades, Julie's friendship remained a source of great joy and happiness. We would always pick up just where we had left off and start laughing and chatting as if no time had even elapsed. Julie's friendship has left its imprint on my soul forever, and my life today is much richer for having crossed paths with her so many years ago.

Cathy and Mary

Another dear friend from my OB nursing days in Omaha was Cathy, who actually was more than a friend; she was a mother figure to several of us single nurses. We referred to her as "Mom," and she was loved and admired as if she had indeed been our biological mother. We worked the night shift together in labor and delivery (L&D) for two years, and during that time, we bonded as if we were blood relatives. Mom Cathy trained me during those long night shifts, and there was no doubt I was learning from the best in the business. She had worked for many decades as an RN in L&D, and there was practically no situation she had not already encountered. Night after night, I was in awe of her wealth of knowledge and quiet confidence as we worked side-by-side to help bring new life into the world. Watching her with our patients, as she soothed their fears and encouraged them through the birthing process, was nothing short of remarkable.

When I was looking for a roommate to share an apartment with, I soon learned that Cathy's daughter Mary was too. Cathy quickly put us in touch with each other, and a short time later, we moved in together. This was another point of connection as Mary and I soon became very good friends. Although living in different states, we have maintained that close relationship to this day and I count her as a "sister of my heart." I am very grateful to have Mary in my life today and grateful to Mom Cathy for connecting us!

Over the years to follow, Cathy continued to play a key role in my life, both as a friend and as an adopted mother. Our phone calls would always end the same way: she would say, "Good-bye, and I love you." This was not a casual or light-hearted bunch of words that just floated off of her tongue—it was conveyed with emotion from a place deep in her heart. Sadly, in 2014, she passed away after heart surgery. But what she left behind for all of us is larger than life. She showed us how to truly love others unconditionally. She was kind, warm, genuine, caring, compassionate, and selfless. I miss her every single day, but I am beyond grateful for the richness she added to my life story and the special friendship that connected us for nearly four decades.

In our last conversation, Mom Cathy and I were talking about someone who has been less than kind to me for many years, and we were trying to sort through it all. She finally concluded, "You know, dear, I don't understand it for the life of me, because you know what? You're really not that hard to love!" And then we chuckled together. Her words still linger in my mind today. I had no idea this would be our last conversation. A month later, she was gone.

Wisconsin Friends

Ginny

In looking back on these friendships in Milwaukee, I see so clearly how they helped me to thrive during the challenging years of raising small children without any support from extended family. Another beloved friend whose friendship I still enjoy to this day was Ginny, a neighbor friend in our Milwaukee suburb near Lake Michigan.

Ginny and I bonded instantly as busy moms who were both raising four children, all who were similar in age. Our kids played together a lot, and we saw each other many days of the week during our carpool pickups, Girl Scout meetings, and play dates. In many ways, those were tough days as we tried to keep up with life and eight busy young children. Although our gal pal time was limited, we never missed an opportunity to laugh and share our funny mommyhood stories with each other. At the time, I had no idea how much our laughter therapy was keeping me afloat. Looking back from where I sit today, I clearly see how sharing those lighthearted moments kept me grounded, encouraged, and sane. I value those phone calls and chats from back then now more than ever.

Chrissy

One of my beloved Milwaukee friends from my time of raising small children was Chrissy, a young Canadian mother who had older children. Chrissy lived across the street, and she would often come over for coffee. Upon seeing how over-whelmed I was, she'd ask, "Which two kiddos can I kidnap today for a sleepover with our kids?" Then out the door she would go, with her children and a couple of mine, to give me a tiny break and a short glimpse of sanity again. Chrissy was my lifeline—she was tossing me a rope when I was drowning in the sea of motherhood.

I have always maintained that this dear friend was a true angel walking among us, and I still believe that to the core of my soul. I have never forgotten what a blessing her friendship was to me during those chaotic times. My hope is that I may honor her by paying it forward to another young mom who needs a rope tossed in her direction as she tries to keep her head above water. Maybe even the words of this book and the ideas and encouragement it offers will serve as a lifeline to women who feel they are swimming upstream in life.

Kari

Another treasured friendship from my eleven years of living in Milwaukee was someone I met while working as a nurse in a highly-skilled-care nursing home. Kari and I would meet for our daily coffee breaks and lunch as often as our busy work schedules would allow. It was fun to have a work buddy and someone to provide a little humor and diversion during the long shifts. We quickly became fast friends, and we contin-ued our special friendship even when I stayed home to be a full-time mom. After I moved to Texas, Kari and I continued to stay in close touch through emails, cards, letters, and calls. We both were dedicated to our friendship, and in spite of our individual obstacles, we never let our friendship suffer. We had a mutual respect for this relationship that spanned many decades and over a thousand miles and we prioritized it. And when I walked across the stage to receive my master's degree in 2001, she was there to cheer me on, something she had promised me she would do years before while I was sweating in the trenches of grad school. We have continued to honor our sisterhood friendship by attending each other's children's weddings, and recently we shared our newest roles as grandmas. I am much richer for having known this special girlfriend and participating in this wonderful bond of enduring friendship. I would sum it up in one word: *priceless*.

Ya-Yas

As the years have flown by, our Ya-Ya sisterhood has become even more priceless. We live in three different states and continue to give priority to our longtime friendships. Today, we are sharing the joys of our children's wedding celebrations and the births of our grandbabies. Life is busy for all of us, and our girlfriend getaways are a rare treat, but we stay in touch regularly nonetheless.

Friendships that began in Milwaukee nearly 40 years ago continue to thrive and feed our souls. Kathy, Beth, Jody, and I look forward to many more Ya-Ya gatherings and treasured moments. We were fortunate to connect again at Beth's son's wedding last summer after five years of being apart. But in true Ya-Ya fashion, we picked right up where we had left off the last time. We shared laughter, love, and hugs, and then we said our good-byes, grateful for the brief time we had to share our sisterhood once again. The Ya-Yas are a true testament to the friendship concept that you can stay closely connected despite geography, separation, and living in a world that moves at a frenetic pace.

Texas Friends

Sharon

In 1992, the move from Milwaukee to Texas brought some new friendships that are still thriving and enriching my life in so many ways. To this day, I am quite amazed by how things just lined up, and special women were placed in my life at just the right moment. I was feeling the pains of transition with the move south, where we knew nobody. But I recognized that God had a plan, and once again, my struggles became easier to deal with and my burdens were lighter. This was because Sharon, a very special lady who was actually our relocation realtor in Houston, very quickly became a friend. Sharon not only assisted us with finding housing, but she came to our rescue—literally—when our family was in a serious car accident on a busy Houston freeway two months after our move.

Our car was in the middle of a seven-car pileup that injured our nine-year-old daughter. We all were taken by ambulance to the emergency room, and we called the only people we knew to save us. This new friend and her husband came to the hospital to help us and took the kids home with them. This allowed my husband and me to tend to his elderly mother and her friend who were severely injured and required immediate surgery.

The next week was a blur as we tried to deal with the aftermath of this accident, but we were blessed beyond words to have this friend in our lives to support us during those traumatic hours (we were very fortunate to all recover from that accident). Sharon continues to be a trusted lifelong friend. I think of her as an angel; she is always there to give of herself to help make the world a better place for others. I hit the jackpot when she came into my life almost 30 years ago, and I honestly do not think I could have survived the challenges of our move to Texas without her love, encouragement, support, advice, and selflessness.

Karen

Another strong sisterhood that began in Texas over two decades ago is a special friendship that encompasses the wild roller-coaster ride of life. Karen and I have been there for each other during some of life's most challenging hurdles. We have bared our souls and shared our fears and most raw parts of our authentic selves. She knows that no matter what, I will have her back, and I know she will have mine. What I think solidifies our friendship is an unspoken loyalty and trust. We have shared many good times as well as some dark days, but when we are together, time seems to stand still, whether we are chatting on the phone or having lunch (and there have been times our lunch dates almost became dinner dates as a result!). I truly see how our special and unique friendship was not an accident—it was God's perfect timing at work.

She holds a special place in my friendship heart, and my life is richer because of her.

Ronda

During the summer of 1995, a new family from Oregon moved in across the street, and they had two boys exactly the same ages as our two boys. It was the beginning of a lasting friendship that still thrives today. The kids bonded immediately and played on the same sports teams through the years. We participated in many family activities together, and we joked that we should build a tunnel under the street to connect our homes and make it easier for everyone to go back and forth. Our husbands became good friends, and we enjoyed sharing time as couples and as families. Most important, the special bond between Ronda and me that began as neighbors and mothers of boys has become a dear and lasting friendship that I treasure.

Friendship Groups

Mom's Group

My husband's career has taken us to four states and eight different cities, and I have been blessed to have made many friendships along this journey. Some of these relationships are still thriving and bringing me great joy today. Others have been wonderful and meaningful friendships that only lasted a few short years or a decade and then faded away. From where I sit today, I can look back on these friendships and see so much good that came from them. Whether it was the group for pregnant moms that I met at our YMCA in Milwaukee or the wonderful neighbor across the street who became my lifesaver when I was isolated and overwhelmed, they all played a unique and special part in my life journey.

Church Group

As I mentioned previously, soon after our move to Texas in 1992, we joined a nearby church that became a rich source of special friendships for our family. I am blessed by these treasured friendships, and my husband, our four adult children, and I continue to enjoy these lasting relationships today, despite the fact that we have moved out of this suburb and are challenged by distance. We share the joys—yes, even the sorrows—of life together. I cannot imagine life without these amazing girlfriends in it. A shout-out to Karen, Twyla, Ellen, Janet, Sue, and Megan for their love and dedication to me and my family through the years. You all have blessed me beyond measure!

The imprint my cherished friendships have left on my soul is permanent, not to be erased by time, and linger long after some of my friends have left to soar with the angels. I am a forever-changed, forever-improved version of myself because of them.

The purpose of sharing these personal stories is to high-light the power of female friendships not only to shape who we become over our lifetime, but to underscore the ability we have as women to impact each other in a lasting way. As we walk the path of life together, we are shaping each other in ways that are not usually acknowledged or easily measured.

Thank you for reading *The Healing Power of Girlfriends*. I hope you've enjoyed reading it as much as I've enjoyed sharing it with you. If you have any questions or comments, I invite you to contact me at http://GalleriaCounseling.com.

Please consider leaving a review wherever you purchased this book—reviews help other readers decide which books to read next, and I would greatly appreciate yours.

I would love to speak to your group or organization. Please contact me at http://www.galleriacounseling.com/contact/, and let's chat.

REFERENCES

Baumeister, R., & Leary, M. (1995). The need to belong: Desire for interpersonal attachments as a fundamental human motivation. *Psychological Bulletin, 117*, 497–529.

Barcella, Laura. (2017, July 24). According to science, your girl squad can help you release more oxytocin. Healthline.com. Retrieved from https://www.health line.com/health/womens-health/benefits-of-a-girl squad-and-female-friendships#1.

Chopik, W. J. (2017). Associations among relational values, support, health, and well-being across the lifespan. *Personal Relationships, 24*(2), 408–422.

Christakis, N. (2009, April 30). The time 100: The world's most influential people. Scientists and Thinkers. *Time Magazine*. Retrieved from http://content.time. com/time/specials/packages/article/0,28804, 1894410_1893209_1893472,00.html

Christakis, N., & Fowler, J. (2009). *Connected: The surprising power of our social networks and how they shape our lives*. New York, NY: Little Brown and Company.

Cook Maher, A., Kielb, S., Loyer, E., Connelley, M., Rademaker, A., Mesulam, M. M., Rogalski, E. (2017). Psychological well-being in elderly adults with extraordinary episodic memory. *PLOS ONE, 12*(10), e0186413. https://doi.org/ 10.1371/journal.pone.0186413.

Diener, E., & Seligman, M. E. P. (2002). Very happy people. *Psychological Science, 13*, 8083.

Diener, E., & Seligman, M. E. P. (2004). Beyond money: Toward an economy of well-being. *Psychological Science in the Public Interest, 5*(1), 131.

Dunkel Schetter, C. (2017). Moving research on health and close relationships forward—A challenge and an obligation: Introduction to the special issue. *American Psychologist, 72*(6), 511–516.

Holt-Lunstad, J., Robles, T. F., & Sharra, D. A. (2017). Advancing social connection as a public health priority in the United States. *American Psychologist, 72*(6), 517–530.

Holt-Lunstad, J., Smith, T. B., & Layton, J. B. (2010). Social relationships and mortality risk: A meta-analytic review. *PLOS MEDICINE, 7*(7), e1000316. https://doi. org/10.1371/journal.pmed.1000316.

House, J.S., Umberson, D., & Landis, K.R. (1988). Structures and processes of social support. *Annual Review of Sociology, 14*, 293–318.

Kelly, M. (2005). *The seven levels of intimacy: The art of loving and the joy of being loved.* Boston, MA: Beacon Press.

Kroenke, C. H., Kubzansky, L. D., Schernhammer, E. S., Holmes, M. D., & Kawachi, I. (2006). Social networks, social support, and survival after breast cancer diagnosis. *Journal of Clinical Oncology, 24*(7), 1105–1111.

Myers, D. G. (2000). The funds, friends, and faith of happy people. *American Psychologist, 55*(1), 56–67.

Nelson, S. (2013). *Friendships don't just happen!: The guide to creating a meaningful circle of girlfriends.* New York, NY: Turner Publishing Company.

Northwestern University. (2017, November 1). *Close friends linked to a sharper memory.* https://news. northwestern.edu/stories/2017/november/close-friends-superager-memory/.

Peterson, Christopher. *A primer in positive psychology.* (2006). New York, NY: Oxford University Press.

Pietromonaco, P. R., & Collins, N. L. (2017). Interpersonal mechanisms linking close relationships to health. *American Psychologist, 72*(6), 531–542.

Ramp, C., Hagen, W., Palsboll, P., Berube, M., & Sears, R. (2010). Age-related multi-year associations in female humpback whales. *Journal of Behavioral Ecology and Sociobiology, 64*, 1563–1576.

Rook, K. S., & Charles, S. T. (2017). Close social ties and health in later life: strengths and vulnerabilities. *American Psychologist, 72*(6), 567–577.

Rubin, G. (2009). *The happiness project.* New York, NY: Harper Collins.

Schnettler, S., & Wohler, T. (2015). No children in later life, but more and better friends? Substitution mechanisms in the personal and support networks of parents and the childless in Germany. *Ageing and Society, 36*, 1339–1363.

Smalley, E., & Oliver, C. (2007). *Grown-up girlfriends: Finding and keeping real friends in the real world.* Carol Stream, Illinois: Tyndale House Publishers, Inc.

Spiegel, D. (November 18, 2014). *How your friends help you live longer* [Video file]. Retrieved from https://www. youtube.com/watch?v=hendwnbSFws.

Suanet, B., van Tilburg, T. G., & Broese van Groenou, M. I. (2013). Nonkin in older adults' personal networks: More important among later cohorts? *The Journal of Gerontology: Series B: Psychological Sciences and Social Sciences, 68,* 633–643.

Taylor, S. E., Klein, L.C., Lewis, B. P., Gruenewald, T. L., Gurung, R. A. R., & Updegraff, J. A. (2000). Female responses to stress: Tend and befriend, not fight or flight. *Psychological Review, 107*(3), 411–429.

ABOUT THE AUTHOR

Deborah A. Olson, RN, MA, LPC, is a women's emotional health specialist. She has provided counseling services for nearly two decades in the greater Houston, Texas, area through Galleria Counseling, her private practice. As a specialist in women's issues, parenting concerns, and marital struggles, she offers life enrichment seminars and retreats and provides hands-on solutions to enhance life in meaningful, purposeful, and emotionally healthy ways. Her workshops are specially designed for women, and topics include depression, anxiety, life transition issues, empowerment, parenting matters, and romantic relationship problems.

As a mother of four adult children, Olson knows firsthand the challenges women face while balancing the many roles of mother, wife, and professional. She is keenly aware of the struggles that couples face in their marital relationships, and after being married for 40 years, she understands the hard work involved in keeping a marriage healthy.

Prior to going into private practice, Olson was a registered nurse specializing in obstetrics and gynecology, labor and delivery, and the newborn nursery. This professional tract has served as a strong foundation for her current career in counseling women, and she has received advanced training and certification in women's emotional health, qualifying her to treat perinatal mood disorders such as postpartum depression and anxiety.

Olson holds a bachelor's degree in psychology from the University of St. Thomas and a master's degree in clinical psychology from Sam Houston State University.

She lives with her husband in a suburb of Houston, Texas. The mother of two daughters and two sons, she is also the proud grandmother of five and a frequent pet sitter for two granddogs. Her favorite leisure activities are spending time at the beach, shelling, boating, traveling, scrapbooking, golfing, writing, and being with her family. Learn more at http://GalleriaCounseling.com.